Open Pages

in South Asian Studies

Also available from SASA Books:

Beginning the Mahābhārata:
A Reader's Guide to the Frame Stories
James W. Earl, University of Oregon

Yaśodā's Songs to her Playful Son, Kṛṣṇa
Lynn Ate, Washington State University

The Multicultural Challenge:
A Visual-Cultural Guide to Coping in the Global Era
Ingrid Aall, California State University, Long Beach

Decoding a Hindu Temple: Royalty and Religion in the Iconographic Program of the Virupaksha Temple, Pattadakal
Cathleen Cummings, University of Alabama, Birmingham

Open Pages in South Asian Studies

Alexander Stolyarov, convenor
Joe Pellegrino, editor

THE RUSSIAN STATE
UNIVERSITY FOR THE HUMANITIES

South Asian Studies Association
Woodland Hills, California
www.sasaonline.net

Published by SASA Books
A Project of the South Asian Studies Association
Woodland Hills, California 91367
A public benefit, non-profit corporation,
EID 26-143783
www.sasaonline.net

Version Control:
1) 15 July 2014

ISBN 978-0-9834472-8-3 (paperback)
ISBN 978-0-9834472-9-0 (electronic, PDF)
LCCN: 2014942506

Cover painting courtesy of William and Judith Vanderbok.

CONTENTS

Preface
William Vanderbok vi

Introduction
Alexander Stolyarov ix

INDOLOGY PAGES

Some Problems in the Study of Old Tamil Literature
Alexander Dubianski 1

Aryan Prehistory and the Indian Civilization
Sergey Kullanda 15

The Prescriptive Function of Language in the *Nyāyamañjarī* and in Speech Act Theory
Elisa Fresci 27

Was there a Chinese Form of Atomism? The *Vaiśeṣika* Atomistic Text in the Chinese Philosophical Tradition
Victoria Lysenko and Artem Kobzev 63

MODERN PAGES

The Western Tribal Region in South Asia:
The Limits of Our Knowledge
Vyacheslav Y. Belokrenitsky 77

Modernity, Diversity, and the Public Sphere:
Religious Identities in 18th-20th Century India.
Some Ideas on Pre-Colonial Modernity:
The Case of the Indian Muslim Pietists
Jamal Malik 111

The Past and Present of Theravada Buddhism
in Sri Lanka: Traditional Heritage v. the
Challenge of Modernity
A.L. Safronova 137

Netaji Subhas Chandra Bose:
His Life and Fate
Tatiana Shaumyan 155

FUTURE PAGES

How to Choose a Good
Indological Problem
Dominik Wujastyk 173

Where Are We Going?
A South Asian Studies Trend Analysis
William Vanderbok 195

PREFACE

WILLIAM VANDERBOK

The 2011 Open Pages in South Asian Studies conference celebrated the launching of Russia's first South Asian Studies program housed at the Russian State University for the Humanities, Moscow. Participants included scholars from Russia, Europe, the United States and India. This volume is dedicated to their budding friendship and continued collaboration.

Without the steady, guiding hand of Dr. Alexander Stolyarov, neither the RSUH program on South Asia nor the Open Pages conference would have been possible. Almost immediately collaboration between the Open Pages participants and the South Asian Studies Association took root. Conference participants Vyacheslav Y. Belokrenitsky, Jamal Malik, Alexandra L. Safronova, Alexander Stolyarov, and William Vanderbok have all subsequently published in SASA's journal, *Exemplar: The Journal of South Asian Studies.*

Finally, the Open Pages conference would have moved forward although the Russian-SASA collaboration would not have been possible but for the timely, critical travel support provided by the American Councils for International Education. Joe Pellegrino and I owe a great debt of gratitude to Dan E. Davidson, President of the American Councils, for his vision in anticipating what was possible.

Dr. William Vanderbok is the President of the South Asian Studies Association, USA.

Dr. Joe Pellegrino is a Associate Professor in the Department of Literature and Philosophy at Georgia Southern University, and editor of ***Exemplar: The Journal of South Asian Studies***, a publication of the South Asian Studies Association.

INTRODUCTION

ALEXANDER STOLYAROV

Open Pages in South Asian Studies: I

While sitting at numerous conferences and workshops and listening to long presentations, I caught myself thinking of the most interesting things that every specialist wished to know:

- How do our close colleagues approach their work?
- What is their mode of working?
- How do they come to their results?
- What questions do they put to the subject of their study?
- What questions can they answer?
- What questions are currently unanswered?
- Why does this current state of affairs exist?

The latter point seemed to me the most important and interesting. Being keen specialists and knowing the subject of their study in depth, our colleagues could present a thorough vision of it: not only what is known, but also what is unknown. To my mind, in our work, to know the borders of the unknown is probably the most important thing that helps us define proper directions for further research.

First of all, this way of addressing our discipline helps to estimate the scale of the problems we are thinking over, link them with other problems, both solved and unsolved, and understand the main reasons that prevent this or that problem from being solved.

That is why and how the idea emerged to make a workshop about such unsolved problems in South Asian studies. It was the International Centre for South Asian Studies of the Russian State University for the Humanities that invited colleagues to discuss the problems of the unknown in their research work. The workshop was entitled "Open Pages in South Asian Studies." It was held at the Russian State University for the Humanities in Moscow on April 27-28, 2011.

The purpose of the workshop was to draw the attention of scholars not to achievements and results, as with our usual academic conferences, but to allow us to focus on problems and questions, to concentrate on details that still remain "blank" or "unrevealed" for this or that reason, whether objective or subjective, deliberately or accidentally. Workshop panelists were asked to explore such "open pages," and this volume presents a collection of articles based on papers delivered at the workshop.

The volume is evenly divided in terms of historical research. The first four papers of the book may be regarded as belonging to "classical Indological" studies, while the next four papers address so-called modern studies. The final two papers consider the discipline as a whole, looking at who we are and how we work. Collectively, the papers included in this book show that the most common reason for "pages" to remain "open" is just the lack of data, the lack of information.

In the "classical" papers here, the common denominator is the problem(s) of origin(s) (or the absence, the non-originating) of various cultural traditions. Thus Alexander Dubianski treats the problem of the origins of Old Tamil poetry. Sergey Kullanda tries to find linguistic data which would shed light on the origin of the *varṇa* system. Elisa Fresci considers the problems of the origin of Mīmāṃsā linguistics. Two historians of philosophy, Victoria Lysenko and Artemiy Kobzev, try to find explanations for the fact that atomistic theories were conspicuously absent in Chinese thought. The authors put forward the hypothesis that the origins of atomism and atomistic thinking are connected with the alphabetic (analytical) principle of writing in India (as in Greece), while in China, with its ideographic writing system, atomism could not be easily evolved and/ or assimilated.

In modern studies the paucity of information is also one of the main problems. It is clearly demonstrated by all the papers of this section. Professor Vyacheslav Belokrenitsky assesses the situation in South Asia's Western Tribal Region. Professor Jamal Malik deals with phenomena of "messianism," "pietism," and "fundamentalism" in "Greater South Asia" from the 16th century until the end of the 20th century. Professor Alexandra Safronova writes about the past and present of Theravada Buddhism in Sri Lanka. Professor Tatyana Shaumyan treats the mystery of the death of legendary Subhas Chandra Bose.

In two papers some theoretical as well as practical questions of South Asian studies in general have been raised. These are, first, the paper of Dominik Wujastyk, who speculates on the prospects for future scholars to find unexplored problems and, second, the paper of Professor William Vanderbok, who analyzes the main trends of South Asian studies in the USA for the last sixty years as compared to European approaches.

The workshop has shown that there is no shortage of both "open pages" in South Asian studies and efforts to explore and "close" them. It is encouraging to observe that nobody tries to stop these efforts. So we may hope for future growth of our discipline.

The workshop participants believe that this book will be interesting not only for specialists and students but also for a wide circle of readers who want to know the history, culture and modern development of the South Asian nations.

Dr. Alexander Stolyarov is a Senior Scientist in the Department of Eastern History at the Institute of Oriental Studies of the Russian Academy of Sciences, Moscow. As Director of Russia's first South Asian Studies program, located at the Russian State University for the Humanities, he organizes the biannual Open Pages conferences in Moscow.

CHAPTER 1

ALEXANDER DUBIANSKI

Some Problems in the Study of Old Tamil Literature

When considering the contribution of Tamilnadu to Indian culture in general we note its many achievements: in the sphere of architecture and sculpture, in the arts of dance, music and many others. But perhaps the most remarkable among them is the corpus of literary works traditionally called "*caṅkam* poetry," rich in volume, aesthetical beauty, and artistic skill. This poetry is nowadays recognized as an indispensable part of the old Indian literary tradition, which is represented mostly in the Sanskrit and Prakrit languages.

The three main branches of this tradition (that is, Sanskrit, Prakrit and Tamil) have much in common, and one of the urgent tasks of research scholars is to understand and explain their interrelation, mutual influence, and development. An overall and coherent picture of the literary processes in ancient India is still to be drawn. Obviously, such a task cannot be solved without fundamental research in each branch of the tradition. From this point of view a research work on Tamil *caṅkam* poetry seems especially important because, in my opinion, this poetry, in spite of the fact that it possesses features of a well-developed and refined art, preserves easily recognizable traces of the early stages of literary development, including elements of folklore. Such a situation makes it possible to follow the development of literary forms, conventions, and canonic images more closely. But one should not forget that studies of Tamil literature represent a comparatively new field of Indological research, and Tamil literature still contains many "open pages" for future scholars. In other words, there are many problems present, concerning the history of Tamil literature, its characteristic features, definitions, estimations etc., which give room for debates and controversies.

There is, for instance, an oft-recurring statement that the old Tamil literature was "rediscovered" at the end of the 19th and the beginning of the 20th centuries by some patriots of Tamil culture (like U.V. Swaminathaiyar, C.V. Damodaran Pillai). As H. Tieken has recently pointed out (*Blaming the Brahmins*, 235), this notion recurs in works by famous scholars like, for instance, A.K. Ramanujan, who gave to one of the chapters of the introduction to translations from *caṅkam* poetry the heading, "A Tradition Lost and Found" (XI). This position was also shared by K. Zvelebil (*Companion*, 147). However, there are different opinions on the subject which take into consideration the fact that though some manuscripts (nobody knows how many) perished in the course of time, the old poetic tradition has certainly survived and, as Tieken correctly states "was never lost" (*Blaming the Brahmins*, 235). Putting aside historical, cultural, and even political reasons for privileging the concept of "rediscovery," I'd like to stress that this tradition had persisted throughout the long middle ages, revealing itself in the form of genres, images, conventions and literary terms.

At the same time we must admit that the so-called "rediscovery" first of all meant the creation of editions of texts which made them known to a large audience and made possible the beginning of their research. The pioneering work on ancient Tamils and their culture was written by V. Kanakasabhai and published in 1904. It was called *The Tamils Eighteen Hundred Years Ago*, and contained a lot of material—geographical, historical, and sociological—extracted mostly from the literary texts. This book was a starting point for a tradition of treating the *caṅkam* poetry as a source of information, a tradition that still exists (mostly in Tamilnadu), though in a modified, more topical, so to speak, form. There are numerous works which present and treat one special object or phenomenon singled out of the poetry. They do not claim to be conceptual, but can be very useful because they collect and present specific facts in a concentrated and systematic way. As one example I offer the monograph by M. Varadarajan, "The Treatment of Nature in Sangam Literature," in which the author describes the objects of nature and gives quotations from the poems. Some authors narrow their field of research to a single-case study. The works by D. Nataraja are also significant in this respect: "*Gloriosa Superba* in Classical Tamil Poetry," and "*Kāmaṉ* in Tamil Classical poetry," among others.

For a scholar who studies ancient Tamil lyrics, works like Sundaramati's "The Theme of *Marutam* in *Caṅkam* Literature" or Ceyeraman's "Neytal Songs," which give carefully collected and rubricated information concerning the themes of old love-poetry, are very good and useful, but they lack an analytical approach from the point of view of the science of literature in the Western sense of the word.

It seems that only in the 1960s were efforts to analyze *cańkam* poetry in terms of the literary theory undertaken. The first work to be mentioned in this connection is *Tamil Heroic Poetry,* by K. Kailasapathy, who tried to place Tamil poetry in the context of world literature, and interpreted it as belonging to the epic tradition (like *The Iliad* or *The Mahabharata*). He stated that Tamil songs belong to the same category of literature and possess its important features: formulas, typical motives, and cycles. It was a new word in Tamilology which produced an impression on scholars, but not all of them accepted it readily. For instance, I supported the idea that the origin of the tradition should be looked for in the situation of oral performance, but could not accept the thesis that Tamil heroic poetry is equal to the epic heroic poems just mentioned. I pointed out that the typical situation in which these poems were composed and sung, their aim and character (they are mostly praise-poems), the mode of performance and the figures of performers, differ considerably from those of the big poems. Tamil poems are not narrative, but mainly descriptive and in principle oriented to the task of praising a person or some events belonging, not to a faraway past, but to a moment more or less contemporary to the performer. In my understanding they formed a part of a certain ritual (a panegyric ritual, let us say) performed jointly by a ruler (a king or a chieftain) and a performer in order to sustain the life-giving power of the ruler on the one hand and the prosperity of the land and the people on the other (*Ritual and Mythological Sources*, 71). The ritual had formed not only the contents of the panegyrics but also influenced their stylistic, poetic features and artistic devices.

In this connection there arises a question: what is the role of rituals or ritual structures in forming the Tamil poetic tradition? As I tried to show, it is possible to consider the main situation of Tamil lyrical poetry (*akam)*, namely, the separation of lovers, in ritual terms, namely as a rite of passage (*Ritual and Mythological Sources*, 138). That is to say, this situation is depicted in poetry as following a certain model of behavior which, when a woman is concerned, is known in Tamil culture as *noṉpu*, or *pāvai noṉpu* (*Ritual and Mythological Sources*, 126-129). This behavior in its turn presupposes the existence of a kind of a feminine energy which was qualified by the American scholar George Hart as *aṉaṅku* (the Tamil word that primarily denotes "suffering, affliction, distress, fear") and called by him, "sacred energy." According to Hart, this energy is immanent in many objects (including humans) and especially important when it is connected with figures of a Tamil king and a woman. Being ambivalent by nature (it is able to give both good and evil), it needs a sort of a control which can be achieved by ritual measures (*The Poems of Ancient Tamil*, 96; *The Relation between Tamil and Classical Sanskrit Literature*, 321).

Hart's theory had garnered some support (for example, Zvelebil's *Tamil Literature* and my own *Ritual and Mythological Sources*), but at the same time was strongly criticized. In his review of Hart's work, T. Burrow pointed out that in early Tamil literature there was no notion of such energetic potential and the word *aṇaṅku* signified spirits, demons, or gods. This critical attitude was strengthened by V.S. Rajam's "Ananku: A Notion Semantically Reduced to Signify Female Sacred Power," where she meticulously collected and analyzed all the contexts where the word was used. She reproached

Hart for presenting an oversimplified, reductionistic interpretation of the term (257). She showed that the "the term *aṇaṅku* does not lend itself to a single interpretation" (250) and that over time it "has undergone a semantic change, a change of a shriveling quality, narrowing from a multi-dimensional concept of a celestial female" (266).

The last statement cannot raise objections, coupled as it is with the recognition that Hart was at times perhaps carried away by his ideas, and had allowed some exaggerations. But it does not prevent us from acknowledging the importance of *aṇaṅku* as the concept of some inner, particularly female, energy. Contrary, though, to Hart's understanding of it as a supernatural power (very much like the Polynesian *mana* (22), I consider this energy as a natural phenomenon, presenting itself in the form of heat or fire (cf. the concept of *tapas*). There are some conspicuous passages in the poetry proving this idea: "thick pieces [of meat] fried (*aṇaṅkiya*) on fire" [from the anthology *akanāṉūṟu* 237, 9], "a fireplace with *aṇaṅku*" (*aṇaṅkaṭuppu)*" [from the poem *maturaikkāñci,* 29]. Another important feature of *aṇaṅku* is its fluctuant nature, an ability to change forms, to be collected or wasted. The best example in this respect will be the figure of Kaṇṇaki, the heroine of the poem *cilappatikāram,* who became a goddess by means of accumulating a huge potential of inner energy which she unleashed in an attempt to burn up the city of Madurai.

In my opinion, the concept of *aṇaṅku* as the inner feminine energy enables us to understand the meaning of images and conventions in Tamil love poetry. For example, specific features of the canonic portrait of the heroine (vegetative code) are aptly explained with the help of it (Dubianski, "Constructing Poetic Images," 90), as well as the whole situation of separation which, as stated earlier, can be viewed as a kind of the ritual of passage. Moreover, this concept offers an interpretation of the meaning and origin of the system of five *tiṇai*, the basic poetic construction of the Tamil love-poetry, which regularly correlates landscapes and love-situations.

The origin of this system was discussed by many scholars, resulting in several with different suppositions. Thani Nayagam suggested a socio-geographical interpretation of this system (88); Sivatamby looked upon it from a socio-economic point of view, stating, for example, that the situation of separation reflects the mode of economic activity of the population of pasture-lands (*passim* in "An Analysis of the Anthropological Significance of the Economic Activities"). There was also the idea of explaining the origin of the five-fold system of landscapes on the basis of five natural elements (*pañcabhuta*) (Zvelebil, *The Smile of Murugan*, 93-95), which looks very artificial. The last attempt was undertaken by Tieken, who suggested that the system of Tamil poetic conventions was inspired by the Sanskrit theory of music (*Kavya in South India*).

Without entering into a discussion of all the suggestions, and recognizing that they all have their convincing points, I shall put forward my hypotheses based on the idea that the feminine energy mentioned above is consubstantial with the energy of nature, its productive and life-giving power. So, the states of the energy of a woman, its aspects, so to say, in different situations (or stages of life) are understood as replicas of the state of nature in different moments of the calendar cycle, or vice-versa. That is why it is not a mere coincidence that the state of a woman suffering in separation and the state of nature during the summer heat are described in poetry by the word *vāṭu,* ("to wither, to dry up").

To make this point more comprehensive, let us turn to the poetic themes. The beginning of the young lovers' romance is connected with the theme-*tiṇai* called *kuṟiñci.* The situation it presupposes is traditionally called *puṇartal* ("a union or copulation"), which contains a paradox, because poets when composing *kuṟiñci* poems avoided descriptions of trysts and depicted scenes around them, that are, in fact, the situation of separation. According to my reading of the theme, its essence consists not in the union itself, but in the concept of union and the readiness of the heroes for it, which addresses their maturity or, to be more precise, their sexual ripeness. This idea is more pronounced with regard to the girl, and it is her inner energy, or *aṇaṅku,* which constitutes the focus of the given theme. This explains, by the way, the origin of its name.

Kuṟiñci (*Strobilanthes*) is a shrub with blue flowers, belonging to mountain areas. Strangely enough, it is mentioned in *kuṟiñci*-poetry only five times, each time in comparison with some other plants (e.g., *mango* or *vēṅkai*-tree). Thus, its presence in this poetic tradition is practically nonexistent. A natural question arises: what made the tradition choose this flower for the name of the *tiṇai*? I think that the explanation is twofold. First of all, it is obvious that the blue color in Tamil culture is associated generally with a woman (*Ritual and Mythological Sources,* 90). The second point seems more interesting. *Kuṟiñci* is known in Tamilnadu as a plant which blossoms only once in twelve years. The marriageable age of a girl in Tamil culture, the age of her "blossoming," is also considered to be twelve years. If we take into consideration the above-mentioned correspondence between the natural and the feminine, the profound symbolic meaning of the flower and the name of the theme will become clear.

The motive of the sexual maturity of the girl is expressed in *kuṟiñci* poetry in two ways. The first is the direct indication of physical changes in her (cf. *Kuṟuntokai* 337):

> The buds of her breasts have blossomed,
> the soft thick hair falls from her head,
> the compact rows of her white teeth are full
> since she has lost her deciduous teeth,
> and a few *cuṇaṅku*-spots have appeared on
> her body.

But the most common way is through a general description of the mountain landscape given at the time when flowers are blossoming, fruits and honey are ripening, the millet is ready for harvesting, and streams and lakes are full of water. Individual details also can be full of meaning. For example, the *vēṅkai* tree (*Pterocarpus*) in *kuṟiñci*-poetry plays the role of the hero's (and the god *Murukaṉ*'s) alter ego, so when the simultaneous blossoming of *vēṅkai* and *mango* (signifying the female principle) is mentioned, there is no doubt that the idea of the union of the heroes (including the matrimonial union) is symbolically introduced. In this way the *kuṟiñci* mytho-poetic landscape, saturated with symbolic meaning, is construed.

This principle is discerned in other *tiṇai*-themes. The heroine of the *mullai* poems (*mullai* is a variety of jasmine) is shown as patiently waiting (*iruttal*) for her husband in the state of ritually controlling and accumulating her inner energy, which signifies her marital chastity (*kaṟpu*), and is symbolically represented in Tamil culture by the white color, the main feature of jasmine. The *pālai* poetry symbolically expresses the dangerous aspect of this process (a potentially disastrous character of the situation of separation). In the theme of *marutam* the heroine is also in a dangerous state, this time in connection with her impurity after the birth of a child. This latter circumstance defines the main idea of the theme, which can be seen as feminine energy in its productive state, connected with progeny and fertility. This idea is aptly expressed by the *marutam*-landscape, the fertile lands of rice and the sugar-cane fields, usually shown in the moments of harvest (*pālai* and *marutam* are trees characteristic of these two landscapes). The last theme, the *neytal* (the theme of the blue lily), is also connected with separation and its sorrows. For the most part it utilizes the situations of other *tiṇais* and uses for its natural background the seascape and images which symbolically express the ideas characteristic for those *tiṇais* (*Ritual and Mythological Sources,* 162-167).

It is worth stressing here that I am considering now only the main, pivotal points of the themes, not touching upon their different topical aspects (like the rivalry between the heroine and the courtesan in *marutam,* for instance, or the feelings of the hero). This very schematic presentation of the main canonical themes of Tamil love poetry aims to show its essential features which tie it with the sphere of myth and ritual (and certainly folklore—another problem of Tamil studies). I maintain that the concept of *aṇaṅku* in the sense of inner feminine energy is able to explain many traditional features of the old Tamil poetry and the formation of its poetic canon. As a final example I shall recall the rule of the famous treatise *Tolkāppiyam,* stating that the heroes of *akam* poetry do not have any other names than their *tiṇai*-names (*tolkāppiyam. poruḷatikāram,* 22). This is an obvious recognition of the fact that the poetry deals not with individuals but with generalized types, which represent models of a certain behavior in certain situations, that is, a ritual behavior. We know well that many rituals are connected with the relationship between the sexes and in the context of Tamil culture with the process of controlling *aṇaṅku*, the female inner energy. Tamil love poetry, no doubt, could not avoid it, and showed situations when this power expressed itself in specific ways, which conditioned the behavior of the heroes of the poetry, thus forming the topical structure of the poems. I also have no doubt that some poetic pieces were actively used during rituals in the form of ritual songs of various melodic types and, perhaps, modes of performance. But this thesis still belongs to one of the open pages of the study of Tamil poetry, and is to be closed by future investigations.

Works Cited

Beck, B.E.F. "Colour and Heat in South Indian Ritual." *Man* 4.4 (1969): 553-572.

Burrow, T. 1979 – T. Burrow. "Review of Hart G.L. *The Relation between Tamil and Classical Sanskrit Literature.* Wiesbaden 1976." *Indo-Iranian Journal* 21 (1979): 4.

Ceyarāman, Nārāyaṇacāmi. *Neytal Pāṭalkaḷ: Ti̲ra̲n̲āyvum Pāṭalkaḷum (Neydal Songs)*. Kumaran̲ Patippaka Veḷiyīṭu, Volume 5. Madurai: Kumaran̲ Patippakam, 1978.

Dubianski, Alexander M. "Constructing Poetic Images in Ancient Tamil Poetry (*Pattuppāttu Anthology*)." *Problems of Indian Philology*. Eds. Gurov, N.V. and S.G. Rudin. Moscow: Moscow: Moscow UP, 1974.

———. *Ritual and Mythological Sources of the Early Tamil Poetry*. Gonda Indological Studies, Volume VIII. Gron-

ingen, The Netherlands: Egbert Forsten, 2000.
Hart, George L. *The Poems of Ancient Tamil: Their Milieu and Their Sanskrit Counterparts*. Berkley: U of California P, 1975.
———. "The Relation between Tamil and Classical Sanskrit Literature." *A History of Indian Literature: Vol. X: Dravidian Literature*. Ed., Jan Gonda. Wiesbaden: Harrassowitz, 1974.
Kailācapati, Ka. *Tamil Heroic Poetry*. Oxford: Clarendon Press, 1968.
Kanakasabhai, V. T*he Tamils Eighteen Hundred Years Ago*. Madras: Higginsbotham, 1904.
Nadarajah, D. "The *Gloriosa Superba* in Classical Tamil Poetry." *Tamil Culture* 11 (1963): 280-90.
———. "*Kāmaṉ* in Tamil Classical Poetry." *Jurnal Pengajan India (Journal of Indian Studies. Kuala-Lumpur)* 1 (1983): 73-87.
Rajam, V.S. "*Aṇaṅku*: A Notion Semantically Reduced to Signify Female Sacred Power." *Journal of the American Oriental Society* 106.2 (1986): 257-272.
Ramanujan, Attipat K. *Poems of Love and War: From the Eight Anthologies and the Ten Long Poems of Classical Tamil*. NY: Columbia UP, 1985.
Sivathamby, Karthigesu. "An Analysis of the Anthropological Significance of the Economic Activities and the Conduct Code Ascribed to Mullai Tinai." *Proceedings of the First International Conference Seminar of Tamil Studies: Kuala Lumpur, Malaysia, April 1966*. Dept. of Indian Studies, University of Malaya, 1968.
Thani, Nayagam X. S. *Landscape and Poetry: A Study of Nature and Classical Tamil Poetry*. Bombay: Asia Publishing House, 1966.
Tieken, Herman J. H. *Kāvya in South India: Old Tamil Caṅkam Poetry*. Gonda Indological Studies Vol. X. Groningen: E. Forsten, 2001.
———. "Early Tamil Poetics between *Nāṭyaśāstra* and

Rāgamālā." *Bilingual Discourse and Cross-Cultural Fertilisation: Sanskrit and Tamil in Medieval India.* Whitney Cox and Vincenzo Vergiani, eds. Pondicherry, India: Inst. Francais de Pondichery, 2013. pp. 69-92.
———. "Blaming the Brahmins." *Studies in History* 26.2 (2010): 227-243.
Varadarajan, M. *The Treatment of Nature in Sangam Literature (Ancient Tamil Literature).* Madras: The South India Saiva Siddhanta Works Publishing Society, 1957.
Zvelebil, Kamil. *The Smile of Murugan: On Tamil Literature of South India.* Leiden: Brill, 1973.
———. *Tamil Literature.* Leiden: Brill, 1975.
———. *Companion Studies to the History of Tamil Literature.* Leiden: Brill, 1992.

Dr. Alexander Dubianski is an Associate Professor in the Institute of Asian and African Studies at Moscow State University.

CHAPTER 2

SERGEY KULLANDA

Aryan Prehistory and the Indian Civilization

The origin of many phenomena of Indian culture can be properly understood only against the background of Aryan prehistory. Thus, the search for an Aryan homeland necessarily involves an analysis of interactions between the Aryans and Indo-Iranians and their neighbors, based on the linguistic data. In what follows below, I shall pass over thoroughly investigated contacts between the Aryans and Finno-Ugrians and focus on less conspicuous facts.

It appears from the analysis of Aryan traditions that Proto-Aryans were the bearers of the steppe archaeological cultures. The latter were characterized, *inter alia*, by the use of handmade pottery, in contrast to the wheel-thrown vessels of the proto-urban cultures of the Near East and South Central Asia. Old Indian ritual texts (for the relevant passages see Rau, 1972) testify that wheel-thrown pottery was considered ritually unclean:

> It (the vessel, *sthālī́*) is made by an Aryan (*āryakr̥tī́*) with [horizontal] parts going upwards (*ūrdhvákapālā*) for the unity with divinity (*sadevatvá*); it is united with the gods (*sádevā*). Yet the vessel (*pā́tra*) made by a potter (*kúlālakr̥ta*) wheel-thrown (*cakrávr̥tta*) is Asuric (*asuryà*). (āryakr̥tī́ *bhavaty ūrdhvákapālā sadevatvā́ ya sā́ hí sádevāsuryàṁ vā́ etát pā́tram· yát kúlālakr̥taṁ cakrávr̥ttaṁ – Maitrāyaṇī-saṁhitā* 1, 8, 3)

> One [vessel] is wheel-thrown (*cakravr̥tta*), the other is non-wheel-thrown (*acakravr̥tta*); the wheel-thrown one is Asuric, the non-wheel-thrown is the divine vessel (*devapātra*). That is why a non-wheel-thrown vessel (*tapanī*) must be made for the Agnihotra. (c*akravr̥ttam anyad acakravr̥ttam anyad yac cakravr̥ttaṁ tad asuryaṁ yad acakravr̥ttaṁ tad devapātraṁ tasmād acakravr̥ttām agnihotratapanīṁ kurvīta – Kāṭhaka-saṁhitā* 6, 3)

The linguistic data imply, however, that the Indo-Iranians contacted with the bearers of Northeast Caucasian and Kartvelian languages. It seems likely that Indo-Iranian **uštra* "camel" (Old Indian *úṣṭra-*, Avestan *uštra-* "id") was borrowed from Pra-Nakh **ŭstuv/jŕe* "bull" – cf. Chechen *stu*, genitive case *steran*, Ingush *ust*, genitive case *istar-o*, Batsbi *psṭu*, genitive case *psṭarĩ*) (O.A. Mudrak, personal communication.) Northeast Caucasian **u̯aran/l-* "camel" (Avar and Lak *warani*, Dargwa *walri*, Lezghi *lawar* "id" – cf. Old Indian *vāraṇá* "wild, dangerous"), **wĕršē* "young bull; male" (Avar *basi* "calf," Chechen and Batsbi *borš* "young bull," Chechen *börša* "male [of species]," Archi *boš-or* "husband; man" – cf. Old Indian *vr̥ṣan-*,

Avestan *varəšna-* "man; male"), **mHädwV* "kind of beverage" (Lezghi *med*, Tabasaran *med*, "treacle, syrup," Andian *medi*, Godoberi *medi* "beer" – cf. Old Indian *mádhu-* "sweet intoxicating drink," Avestan *maδu-* "berry wine," Sogdian *mδw* "wine," etc.) were Indo-Iranian loanwords (Klimov 1971: 228; Starostin 1988: 113-114.) Georgian-Zan (a branch of Kartvelian) **rdo-* "time; timespan" (Georgian *dro*, Megrelian *rdo-*; cf. Old Indian *r̥tú-* "fixed time; period," Avestan *ratu-* "timespan"), Georgian-Zan **bandγ-* "to tie, plait" (Georgian *bandγ-* "to tie, to net, to spin webs;" Megrelian *bondγ-* "id"; cf. Old Indian *bandh-*, Avestan *band-* "to tie, bind"), etc. were borrowed from Indo-Iranian (Климов 1994: 176-177; 93-95).

The Indo-Iranians, Northeast Caucasians and Kartvelians could have interacted either in the Near East, before the Indo-Iranians moved to the steppes, or in the Caucasus if they followed the Caucasian way north.

To study the origin of the *varṇa* system, one also has to look into Indo-Iranian and even Indo-European prehistory. Besides the famous *Puruṣasūkta* story (RV X, 90, 11-12), Vedic texts provide very little information on the matter. They imply, however, that the *kshatriya* social class charged with warring and political power bears traces of the age class of young men. The relevant data, collected and analyzed by Stig Wikander (1938, *passim*), can be amplified. Thus, the Vedic Indra, a king and warrior par excellence, is depicted in the Rigveda as an unageing (*ajuryá*) youth (*yúvan*) and *márya*. One can, without stretching the point, trace all the above meanings to a protolanguage etymon marking membership in an age-sex group of young warriors. The latter were likely to be a nuisance in peacetime, hence the meaning "rascal." In time of war, however, they constituted the main military force and, after performing the required warlike deeds, were allowed to enter the next age-grade and marry. Let us see if Indra and the Maruts as described in the Rigveda can be regarded as such a group.

The Maruts in the *Rigveda* are youths (*yúvānas* and *máryās*) mentioned exclusively as a group (*śárdha, gaṇá* or *vrā́ta*) without any individual characteristics. They were born simultaneously (*sākáṁ jajñire* [I, 164, 4]; *sākáṁ jātā́ḥ* [V, 55, 3]), they are of the same nest (*sánīḷāḥ* [I, 165, 1; VII, 56, 1], neither senior nor junior and middle- (*té ajyeṣṭhā́ ákaniṣṭhāsa udbhídó 'madhyamāso...* [V, 59, 6]). They are equipped with the full panoply of weapons, namely battle-axes, spears, bows, arrows, quivers, helmets as well as with horses and chariots (*vā́śīmanta r̥ṣṭimánto manīṣíṇaḥ sudhánvāna íṣumanto niṣaṅgíṇaḥ / sváśvā stha suráthāḥ...svāyudhā́...*, i.e. "[ye are] battle-axe bearers, spearmen, wise, bearers of good bows, arrow-bearers, quiver-bearers; [ye] are possessing of good horses, good chariots... well-armed" [V, 57, 2]. They have gilt helmets on their heads (*śíprāḥ śīrṣásu vítatā hiraṇyáyīḥ* [V, 54, 11]) and mighty bows and (other) weapons in their chariots (*sthirā́ dhhánvāny ā́yudhā ráthesu vó...* [VIII, 20, 12]).

According to the *Rigveda*, the Maruts are *sāṁtapanā́* [VII, 59, 9], that is, as Renou (1962: 46) put it, born of the total burn, *nés de la brûlure-totale*. However, since the prefix *sam-* (here in the *vr̥ddhi* form with a long vowel, *sām-*) implies the action of several agents one is entitled to interpret the word *sāṁtapanā́* as "those who passed through a common ordeal by fire" being an integral part of initiation rites.

A very interesting mention of Indra as a merchant (*vaṇíj*) in the Atharvaveda (*índram ahám vaṇíjaṁ codayāmi*, "I incite Indra the merchant" – XV 15, 1) that at first sight seems to be contradictory to his image of the war chief is in fact quite in keeping with it. Archaic trade was closely related to warring – suffice it to remember the Vikings who were both warriors and traders. This ambiguity was reflected in Indo-European languages where words meaning "war booty" (Sanskrit *lotra*) and "gain, profit" (Latin *lucrum*) go back to the same protolanguage etymon. A classic case of this situation is the image of Wodan, the Germanic war god who was at the same time the protector of trade and in this capacity was identified with Mercury, the god of commerce in Roman mythology. As a result, the day of Mercury in Romance languages (French *mercredi*, etc.) became the day of Wodan (Dutch *woensdag*, English *Wednesday*).

I think that the above materials enable one to trace the Kshatriya *varṇa* to the age-class of young warriors. Unfortunately, we have no information on the relation of the other two primary *varṇas* to age-sex classification in Indian tradition – at least I have not succeeded in unearthing it – but in this case it is Iranian tradition that helps us. Thus, according to a Scythian legend or myth recorded by Herodotus, (IV, 5-7), the Scythian progenitor, Targitaos, had three sons: Lipoxaïs, Arpoxaïs, and the youngest (υεοώτατος) Colaxaïs. As the youngest brother succeeded in getting hold of sacred objects fallen from the sky, the elder brothers ceded the royal power to him. The story goes that "From Lipoxaïs originated those Scythians who are called the clan (γένος) of Auchatae; from Arpoxaïs, those called Katiari and Traspians; from the youngest the kings called Paralatae" (Herodotus IV, 6). Evidently the social position of the three brothers has nothing to do with their birth-order, or the second son would have become the ancestor of kings. Neither can it be a mere error of Herodotus, since in an independent Iranian tradition, that of the Middle Persian Bundahišn, it is the youngest son of Zardusht that becomes the ancestor of the warriors, resp. kings, while the eldest son is the ancestor of priests, and the second son – the ancestor of agriculturalists. Moreover, parts of a system cannot be separated arbitrarily. If one of the social classes was related to an age class, the other two probably had the same origin.

Both Dumézil in 1930 and Grantovskij in 1960 argued that Scythian clans (γένεα) had been social groups going back to age classes (Brandenstein 183-ff.) It was E.O. Berzin who took the logical next step and suggested that Indian *varṇas* had originally been age-classes of young warriors, mature men providing agricultural goods, and old men performing religious duties (Berzin 46). Unfortunately, the works by Brandenstein and Berzin contained, besides convincing arguments in favor of the role of age-sex stratification in the formation of the *varṇa* system, a number of far-fetched statements and outright errors,[1] hence they were greeted with skepticism. Berzin's paper, moreover, was published in a popular magazine, and was thus overlooked by scholarly community. It is therefore appropriate to reiterate and amplify their arguments.

It seems likely that the Kshatriyas were originally warlike youths, the Vaishyas were mature men—having ceased to be warriors *par excellence* and charged mainly with farming and animal husbandry—and the Brahmans belonged to the age-class of elders performing priestly functions. It is all the more probable since there are mentions of age-sex classification in Vedic literature. Thus, the word *váyas* "vigor, strength" means in certain contexts "a stage of life." One can cite such passages from the *Rigveda* as "passing through one life period (*váyas*) after another" (*váyo-vayo vicarántaḥ*)

[VIII, 55. 4], "[Soma] circulates through life stages" (*pári... váyāṁsi... yāti*) (IX, 9. 1) or "when thou [i.e. Agni] growest old establishing one life stage after another, / thou goest circle-wise changing thy outlook" (*váyo-vayo jarase yád dádhānaḥ / pári tmánā víṣurūpo jigāsi*) (V, 15. 4), etc.

It is likely that here Agni and Soma personify the movement of human beings through life periods; when an age-group reaches the limit of the socially active age it leaves the system of age-classes and is substituted by a new group assuming its name, that is, the circle-wise movement mentioned in the above-cited passages takes place. As to the age-grades in Vedic tradition, it is worth noting that in the *Śatapatha Brāhmaṇa* (XII, 9, 1, 8) one encounters the word váyas meaning approximately "the active life, vigorous age" and *-vayasá* "life period" in such compounds as *pūrvavayasá-*, *madhyamavayasá-,* and *uttamavayasá-,* meaning the first, middle, and last stage of life, respectively. Let us cite this very instructive passage: "There are three sacrificial cakes, for this life (*váyas*) of man (*púruṣa*) consists of three parts. It is his life that [*adhvaryú*] wins for him by [means of] those [cakes]. The early life (*pūrvavayasá*) [he wins] by that of Indra, the middle [part of] life (*madhymavayasá*) by that of Savitar, and the last [part of] life (*uttamavayasá*) by that of Varuṇa. Having won the life from Death in the sequence [of its periods and] deities [*yajamāna*] makes it immortal" (*tráyaḥ puroḍā́śā bhavanti / tredhāvihitáṁ vā idaṁ púruṣasya váyaḥ / váya évāsyá taíḥ spr̥ṇoti / pūrvavayasámévaindréṇa / madhymavayasáṁ sāvitréṇa / uttamavayasáṁ vārunéṇa / yathārūpámevá yathādevatáṁ váyo mr̥tyóḥ spŕ̥tvāmŕ̥taṅ kurute.*)

All these and many other facts can only be explained as the result of the evolution of an age-stratified society, all the more so since linguistic analysis is indicative of the existence of age-sex stratification in Proto-Indo-European community. I dwelt at length on this issue in my paper ("Indo-European 'Kinship Terms' Revisted"), so here I will confine myself to broad outline of my arguments.

The analysis of Indo-European kinship terminology implies that Proto-Indo-European society was characterized by age-sex stratification. There are about twenty PIE etyma regarded, in accordance with the meaning of the majority of their reflexes, as kinship and relationship-by-marriage (affinal) terms. The reconstructed PIE kinship-terms system is therefore usually divided into two subsystems:

a. consanguineous or blood-kinship terms and
b. affiliation or relationship-by-alliance terms.

In doing so, however, one imposes on the society whose language one is trying to reconstruct one's own perception of kinship, notwithstanding conflicting evidence.

Thus, PIE **bhréh$_2$tēr* is traditionally included into the blood-kinship terms subsystem with the meaning "(consanguineous) brother." It is, however, at the same time traditionally and appropriately considered a designation of any male member of the community/ extended family belonging to the ego's generation, and rightly so.[2] Nevertheless, the obvious discrepancy is tacitly ignored.

It appears that early Indo-European social structure was based on age-sex stratification, with classificatory kinship playing only a secondary role.

The obvious socio-cultural implication of this conclusion is that age-sex stratification underlay the classificatory and individual kinship patterns and may therefore have been the first stage of social evolution that under certain circumstances could have evolved into the *varṇa* system. Yet while the remnants of age-sex classification had survived in a number of the recorded Indo-European traditions, it was among the Indo-Iranians that it evolved into the *varṇa/pištra* system). What circumstances, then, were favorable to the formation of such a system?

There is also the question of where and when it emerged. Given that (1) age-sex stratification is mostly viable among pastoralists, and, more specifically, among those pastoralists who are not exactly nomadic but not quite settled, so to speak, as the Maasai, Gikuyu, Oromo, and other peoples of East Africa (the classical area of age-sex stratification), (2) the Vedic Indians considered wheel-thrown (*cakravr̥tta*) pottery unknown to the bearers of the steppe pastoralist cultures unfit for ritual purposes, and (3) the Indo-Iranians contacted with the Finno-Ugrians of the West Siberian forest zone, it seems likely that the Proto-Indo-Iranians were primarily cattle-breeders inhabiting the steppes of Western Siberia and South Urals.

Thus, the correlation of linguistic evidence and narrative sources gives us an insight into Indo-Iranian prehistory, and, hopefully, into the origin of Indo-Iranian social stratification.

Notes

1. Thus, Brandenstein held that the Scythian γένεα were related to the subsequent inhabitants of the North Pontic area, i.e., the bearers of the Tripolye archaeological culture, resp. the descendants of the elder brother, the bearers of the battle-axe culture, resp. the descendants of the middle brother, and the Scythians proper,

resp. the descendants of the youngest brother, which does not seem likely. Berzin, in his turn, argued that the Indo-Europeans had been mounted warriors while horseback riding was not widespread even in the Indo-Iranian epoch.

2. See Abaev 438-439; Trubachev 58-ff.; Benveniste vol. I: 213-214; Benveniste and Lallot 170-171; Szemerényi 23-24; and Gamkrelidze and Ivanov 764 (666 in their English version).

Works Cited

Abaev, V.I. *Istoriko-Etimologicheskii Slovar' Osetinskogo Iazyka*, vol. I-V. Moscow-Leningrad: Izdatel'stvo Akademii nauk SSSR [Nauka], 1958-1995.

Benveniste, Emile. *Le Vocabulaire Des Institutions Indo-Européenes*. Paris: Les Editions de Minuit, 1969.

Benveniste, Émile, and Jean Lallot. *Indo-European Language and Society*. Coral Gables, FL: U of Miami Press, 1973.

Berzin, E.O. "Sivka-Burka, Veshchaia Kaurka, ili Drevniaia Evropa v zerkale mifov i skazok." *Znanie–sila* 11 (1986).

Brandenstein, Wilhelm. *Griechische Sprachwissenschaft*. Berlin: W. de Gruyter, 1954.

Dumézil, Georges. *La Préhistoire Indo-Iranienne Des Castes*. Paris: P. Geuthner, 1930.

Gamkrelidze, T.V., and V.S. Ivanov. 1984 /1995. *Indoevropeiskii Iazyk i Indoevropeitsy. Rekonstruktsiia i Istoriko-Tipologicheskii Analiz Praiazyka i Protokul'tury*. Tbilisi: Izdatel'stvo Tbilisskogo Universiteta, 1984.

———. *Indo-European and the Indo-Europeans. A Reconstruction and Historical Analysis of a Proto-Language and a Proto-Culture*. Trans. Johanna Nichols. Ed. Werner Winter. NY: Berlin: Mouton de Gruyter, 1995.

Grantovskij, E.A. *Indoiranische Kastengliederung bei den*

Skythen. Moskau: Verlag für Orientalische Literatur, 1960.

Klimov, G.A. "Kavkazskie Ètimologii." *Ètimologiia 1968*. Moscow: Nauka, 1971. pp. 1-8.

———. "O Nekotorykh Slovarnykh Obshchnostiakh Kartvel'skikh i Nakhsko-Dagestanskikh Iazykov." *Ètimologiia 1970*. Moscow: Nauka, 1972. pp. 349-355.

———. *Drevneishie Indoevropeizmy Kartvel'skikh Iazykov*. Moscow: Nasledie, 1994.

Kullanda, Sergey. "Indo-European 'Kinship Terms' Revisited." *Current Anthropology* 43.1 (2002).

Rau, Wilhelm. *Töpferei und Tongeschirr im Vedischen Indien*. Wiesbaden: Franz Steiner Verlag GMBH, 1972.

Starostin, S.A. "Indoevropeisko-Severnokavkazskie Izoglossy." *Drevniĭ Vostok: Ètnokul'turnye Sviazi*. Eds. G.M. Bongard-Levin and V.G. Ardzinba. Moscow: Nauka, 1988. pp. 112-163.

Szemerényi, Oswald. *Studies in the Kinship Terminology of the Indo-European Languages. With Special Reference to Indian, Iranian, Greek, and Latin.* (*Acta Iranica* 16). Téhéran-Liège: Édition Bibliothèque Pahlavi. Leiden: Brill, 1977.

Trubachev, O.N. *Istoriia Slavianskikh Terminov Rodstva i Nekotorykh Drevneishikh Terminov Obshchestvennogo Stroia*. Moscow: Izdatel'stvo AN SSSR, 1959.

Wikander, Stig. *Der Arische Männerbund. Studien zur Indo-Iranischen Sprach- und Religionsgeschichte*. Lund: Håkan Ohlssons Buchdruckerei, 1938.

Dr. Sergey Kullanda is a Senior Scientist in the Department of Ancient Orient at the Institute of Oriental Studies of the Russian Academy of Sciences, Moscow.

CHAPTER 3

ELISA FRESCHI

The Prescriptive Function of Language in the *Nyāyamañjarī* and in Speech Act Theory[1]

The title of the workshop organized by Alexander Stolyarov and of the consequent volume invites me to consider the problem of "what to do first": the problem of priorities. Why do we need priorities? Because *ars longa, vita brevis*—"art is long and life is short"; we have to acquire many skills and our time is limited. Hence, no matter how much we would like to do it, we will not be able to read all the 20 millions of Sanskrit manuscripts waiting to be edited.

Priorities are needed not just for practical purposes (lack of time) or theoretical purposes (a desire to focus on more significant texts), but even for historical purposes. For instance, no one could start her study of the linguistics of the Prābhākara branch of the Mīmāṃsā school with Prabhākara's texts, which are hardly intelligible in themselves. Before reaching Prabhākara, one should rather focus on texts which might, by contrast, be able to spread light on the others. Hence, setting priorities is a fundamental task.

I will focus here on priorities in Classical Indian philosophy, especially in Classical Indian philosophy of language and linguistics.

Priorities in Classical Indian Linguistics

If we leave behind the treatises on Phonetics (the *Prātiśākhyas*), which are highly technical and focused on the specific topic of the accurate pronunciation of Vedic mantras, and Yāska's *Nirukta*, which deals with semantics and has greatly influenced many fields of Indian culture, but has not originated a distinct school,[2] we are left with two kinds of sources for classical Indian linguistics:

- *padaśāstra* ("Teaching about words": mainly Grammar)
- *vākyaśāstra* ("Teaching about sentences": mainly Mīmāṃsā)

The first group badly needs further studies to detect its complex approach and possibly to discern the distinct voices of its authors. Although much work has been done by Ashok Aklujkar, Saroja Bhate, George Cardona, Madhav Deshpande, Ram Nath Sharma, to name only a few, we are in fact still far from mastering the intricacies of Pāṇini's grammar and to be able to have a solid grasp on the entire tradition he founded.

An intermediate condition is the one of studies on the linguistics of Nyāya and Buddhist epistemology, on which some high quality work has been produced, although much remains to be investigated.[3] These two fields of study have in fact benefited from the quality and quantity of scholars focusing on Nyāya and on Buddhist epistemology.

Due to the paucity of scholars focusing on Mīmāṃsā,

by contrast, the study of the second group of texts has hardly been undertaken, and the intricacies of its system are yet to be discovered.[4] Hence, in the context of an "Open Pages" workshop, one cannot help but highlight the need for studying Indian sentence-linguistics. But is the need to study *vākyaśāstra* only linked to the historical reconstruction of Indian thought? Or are there further reasons at all to focus on sentence-linguistics?

The question is generally linked to the problem of the purpose of studying the Sanskrit heritage. One might suggest that all human products are worth preserving (as argued by Jan Houben in his *Appeal to Safeguard Ideo-Diversity*, in Squarcini 2002). But this brings one back to the initial problem, i.e., the necessity of setting priorities. Now, Sanskrit thought particularly excelled in the field of linguistic and philosophy of language. As for *padaśāstra*, Western linguistics has reached the high level of abstraction of Pāṇini's grammar only in very recent times (see Keidan 2011) and, one might add, only after having been fertilized by it (see Alfieri forthcoming). Sentence-linguistics is a field where Indian linguistics may ask thought-provoking questions, add insightful solutions, and display a complex and accurate system of linguistic analysis. Furthermore, the sentence-context is fundamental in order to deal with complex linguistic phenomena, such as deixis, textual linguistics, investigation on the minimal elements of signification, but its study has only recently been undertaken in the West.

In the following, I will especially focus on one of such phenomena, exhortation. In fact, in Western linguistics and epistemology, exhortation is usually considered just an exception to the informative use of language. Even where language is described as having various functions (see Copi and Cohen 1986, chapter 4.1.1–3), the exhortative function is hardly dealt with at all. By contrast, Mīmāṃsakas especially focus on exhortation, as will be explained below.

Having thus established that the study of *vākyaśāstra* is worthwhile, let me now turn to the question of how to go about doing it. To begin with, which sources can one count on?

Unfortunately, there are several problems with the sources for *vākyaśāstra* (problems which mostly apply to all other fields of Indian Philosophy):

- Sanskrit texts were meant mostly for insiders: In India, self-learning is generally condemned (cf. the *Mahābhārata* story about Ekalavya, who has learnt archery by secretly watching Droṇa's lessons).
- Classical texts (and even more so, post-Classical ones) mostly adjust presupposed definitions, rather than explaining them anew.
- We lack the background considered to be the most obvious one: ritual. In fact, in most cases Mīmāṃsā texts presuppose the knowledge of rituals and use ritual examples as explanatory tools. By contrast, we tend to be able to understand examples only once we have understood what they should exemplify.

Before discussing these problems through the analysis of the specific case of exhortation, I shall address the nature of "exhortation."

A Case Study: Exhortation

By "exhortation" I mean the linguistic phenomenon of inducing an effect in the listener/reader. A standard Indian example of exhortation is "the one who is desirous of cattle should sacrifice with the citrā-ritual" (*paśukāmaś citrayā yajeta*). A more common one is "Give me a glass of water." Exhortation is, hence, distinguished from description. The latter includes all statements regarding states of affairs, such as, "Having much cattle means being rich" or "Drinking water is healthy."

Exhortation in Mīmāṃsā

Exhortation is of chief importance for Mīmāṃsā authors, due to their focus on the *Brāhmaṇas*. These are the prescriptive part of the *Vedas*, i.e., the parts of the *Vedas* which contain all sorts of sacrificial injunctions. Since Mīmāṃsā authors developed their linguistics theories in accordance with their focus on the exegesis of the Brāhmaṇas, they regarded the exhortative function as the fundamental function of language. In the next stage, Mīmāṃsā authors extended their theories beyond the *Vedas* and—especially the Prābhākara branch of Mīmāṃsā—argued also that ordinary language is primarily prescriptive. As evidence they mention the process of language acquisition. This does not occur through the descriptive use of language. Children could listen to adults uttering descriptive sentences for an unnaturally long time before they would be able to single out the meaning of single words. By contrast, the experience of exhortative sentences such as "Fetch the cow!" and of the consequent action makes the child easily understand what is going on. Through repeated experience of similar sentences, in which new words are inserted or deleted (e.g., "Tie the cow!" or "Fetch the horse!"), they will learn the language.[5]

One might suggest that in order to study exhortation the tools of *padaśāstra* are enough. An exhortative sentence would be one where an optative, imperative, subjunctive or gerundive verbal ending is found. But this is not correct. Verbal endings are not enough to identify an exhortative sentence, since there are exhortations even in the case of indicative verbal endings and only a sentence-context allows one to detect them. Since their linguistic theories depend on exegetical concerns, Mīmāṃsakas were well aware of this phenomenon and developed theories which took into account the larger context. For instance, in the context of the prescriptions regarding the Darśapūrṇamāsa sacrifice, a statement such as "The sacrificial spoon is made of parṇa wood" means, in fact, "One should use a parṇa-spoon for the present sacrifice." Similarly "I am thirsty" may mean "Please, give me a glass of water," in an appropriate context.[6]

Exhortation and Speech Act theory

By contrast, linguistic studies developed in the West having in view the "scientific" usage of language, i.e., its referential usage.[7] In the 20th century, however, the Western approach to non-descriptive statements received important contributions. A notable example is Roman Jakobson (1896–1982), who deals with the referential function along with other five (expressive, conative, poetic, phatic and metalingual). Among them, the conative function highlights the exhortative aspect of language. Further, in the last decades, the approach to exhortation has been modified through J.L. Austin's Speech Act theory (whose fundamental book is *How to Do Things with Words*, published posthumously in 1962). This analyzes language from the point of view of its pragmatic effects and distinguishes a locutionary, illocutionary, and perlocutionary aspect in it. Noteworthy is also Austin's successor, Searle. Thus, through Jakobson, Austin, and his successor, J.R. Searle, 20th-century linguistics "discovered" non-referential usages of language.

Speech act theory distinguishes the following types of speech acts:

- A locutionary act comprises the act of uttering a sentence and its phatic and rhetic aspects.[8] Austin defines it as the act of using words "as belonging to a certain vocabulary [...] and as conforming to a certain grammar, [...] with a certain more or less definite sense and reference" (Austin 1975, pp. 92-3). The locutionary act is needed in order to distinguish between cases where the locutionary act is the same, but the illocutionary or perlocutionary ones differ. For instance, "I will do everything by myself" could be a constative speech-act, express a threat, a regret...
- Illocutionary speech acts are the core of the theory: they could be of various sorts (greeting, baptizing...) and their characteristic is the fact that they actually perform what they seem to be describing (e.g., a priest telling to a couple "I declare you husband and wife" is not describing a state of affairs which would have existed independently of the statement itself; it rather performs it).
- A perlocutionary act consists of the effect of the illocutionary one (persuading, scaring...).

In a short formulation, "Austin [...] distinguishes the act of saying something, what one does in saying it, and what one does by saying it" (Bach 2006, p. 150). For instance, the bar keeper says "The bar closes in five" (locutionary act). Illocution: urging (to go soon). Perlocution: ordering a last drink.

Within this theory, exhortations are a sub-set of illocutionary speech acts, namely "directive illocutionary speech acts."

To whom does the illocutionary force belong?

Answers from Speech Act theory and Classical Indian linguistics: It is apparent that the Speech Act theory focuses on the role of the speaker. Locutionary and illocutionary acts, in particular, depend on what the speaker does while speaking, while perlocutionary acts regard the effect of the speaker's statements on the listener. By contrast, Mīmāṃsā theories must avoid referring to any speaker, since the paradigmatic instance of language they aim at explaining, the *Veda*, is thought to exist independently of any author. If we leave the historical origin of the *Veda* out of the picture, its author is *now* epistemologically irrelevant, so that it is impossible to claim that the illocutionary power of the *Veda* depends on him/her. In fact —Mīmāṃsā authors claim— one recognizes the authority of the Veda independently of its author, and one does not respect the Veda because of the alleged author of a certain section, but rather because the Veda in itself enjoins an absolute authority. It can be incidentally noted that this was possibly the standard stance in regard to the Veda until theism became the regular option (see McCrea forthcoming).

Thus, although one could be tempted to say that exhortation as seen in Mīmāṃsā is an "illocutionary force," like the one present in commands, Mīmāṃsā authors do not attribute any role to the speaker. This seems to oppose the whole theory of speech acts, since this originates from the observation of the performative use of some verbs and exhortations are classified as directive illocutionary speech acts insofar as a speaker can utter sentences such as, "I order you that...." Furthermore, from the *vākyaśāstra* point of view, the distinction between illocutionary speech acts (intended by a speaker to produce a certain effect) and perlocutionary ones (producing effects on the hearer) is hardly possible. From a certain point of view, a prescription (*vidhi*) is a "perlocutionary force," since it is recognized through its effects on the listeners, rather than through the intention of its speaker. However, according to the Mīmāṃsā standpoint, an exhortation cannot be easily identified through its effects either, since its output is the *undertaking* of an activity and not the activity itself. Thus, its effects are hardly perceivable, if not by the listener himself.

In other words, Classical Indian *vākyaśāstra* focuses on the characteristics of the exhortative function of language itself. This view has the advantage of accounting for cases of exhortations with no speaker, such as the Veda.

I am not aware of any version of the Speech Act theory which does not take into account the role of the speaker. The role of perlocutionary speech acts seems to only regard the description of the *effects* of an act which must have in it an illocutionary force.

In *How to Do Things with Words*, the distinction between illocution and perlocution was chiefly aimed at distinguishing between the meaning intended and the one achieved. Perlocution was never thought of as the *only* aspect of a Speech Act. Searle (Searle 1969) plays down even more the role of perlocution, insofar as he understands it as just an additional element, since "the intention of achieving a perlocutionary effect is not essential to the illocutionary act" (Sbisà 2009, p. 235). Further, perlocution identifies only (external) effects, and seems, therefore, unsuitable to account for exhortations, which seem to be more than just their result on a listener. Also, these appear to have a standard way of functioning, unlike the variety of their perlocutionary effects:

> The performance of a perlocutionary act does not depend on the satisfaction of conventional conditions, but on the actual achievement of a certain goal or (since a perlocutionary act can also be performed unintentionally) on the speech act's having actually caused certain extralinguistic consequences (Austin 1962: 107).[9]

Can the Speech Act theory be modified in order to emphasize the role of the listener alone? Apart from the Veda, such an approach could be used to explain the case of laws, which have an "illocutionary" power that does not depend on their author.

If relying on the listener alone is not a viable solution, one is left only with language. But how can a *force* inhere in a non-sentient thing like language? We shall see later how this point is central for the Indian *vākyaśāstra*, which indeed focuses on the following question: What makes *language* able to convey a perlocutionary effect? Thus, whereas, as already hinted at, the definition of exhortation according to its speaker or listener depends on something outside it, Classical Indian *vākyaśāstra* focuses on some characteristics of language itself.

To sum up, once we have admitted that the role of the speaker might be reduced, we might ask:

> Is language in itself able to convey a perlocutionary effect or does it depend on its listeners in order to attain its purpose? (1)[10]

As far as similar questions are concerned, Classical Indian *vākyaśāstra* could fruitfully interact with Speech

Act theorists. By "interact" I mean that the process ought to be bi-directional, since both interlocutors can enhance their knowledge through the dialogue. Apart from contemporary *vākyaśāstra*-exponents, scholars of Indian linguistics working on *vākyaśāstra* are also included in this suggestion.[11] But, in order to interact, they should be able to understand each other, and this is not always smooth in the case of most Indian sources for exhortation.

Classical Indian Sources

The first and foremost source for the study of exhortation within the Indian *vākyaśāstra* should be Kumārila Bhāṭṭa (beginning of the second half of the first millennium CE), since he is the chief author of the Bhāṭṭa Mīmāṃsā.

Kumārila labels the exhortative force *śabdabhāvanā* "the [force] causing [an action] to be [and] consisting of language." Much about this force is obscure, starting with the controversial analysis of the compound, which can be analyzed as a *karmadhāraya* (i.e., an attributive compound, 'a force causing to be which is language') or as a tatpuruṣa (i.e. 'a force of language'). Whatever its etymology, the name *śabdabhāvanā* evokes a previous author, i.e., Śabara (the first commentator of the root-text of Mīmāṃsā, before the V c. CE). Śabara defines action as *bhāvanā*, i.e., 'causing [a result] to be'.

Kumārila's definition of the two bhāvanās sounds as follows:

> *abhidhābhāvanām āhur anyām eva liṅādayaḥ | arthātmā bhāvanā tv anyā sarvākhyāteṣu gamyate ||*

> The verbal endings of optative, etc., express the designation *bhāvanā*. The bhāvanā consisting of a purpose is, by contrast, something else, and it is understood in the case of all verbal endings (TV ad 2.1.1, Abhyankar and Jośī 1971-1980).

Within the Bhāṭṭa Mīmāṃsā, all later definitions of the *śabdabhāvanā* follow along the same lines. Consider, for instance, Mahādeva Vedāntin's one:

> [...] the productive force based on the word (*śabdabhāvanā*) is denoted by the suffix in the form of the optative, and is established by the experience 'The veda instigates me'(Mahādeva Vedāntin 2010, p. 368).[12]

Here, there is the interesting addition of the experience of being enjoined, but the definition is still far from being clear and understandable.

It can be even worse than that, since in most cases Kumārila's definition is presupposed and the authors just elaborate on it.[13]

Maṇḍana Miśra,[14] who dedicated a whole treatise on exhortation (the Vidhiviveka 'Discernment about prescriptions'), is highly insightful, but his terse style and the lack of reliable editions make the text often obscure. The following lines are the first ones of the Vidhiviveka (the first "it" must refer to the prescriptive force, the second one to the linguistic element and the third to the meaning):

> It is in fact a sort of linguistic element, or an additional function of it, or a sort of meaning. And the linguistic element is also called like that because it designates it.[15]

The situation might improve, though, if one reads

later primers, such as Laugākṣi Bhāskara's *Arthasaṅgraha*:

The linguistic force is a particular activity of someone who causes to be an undertaking of an activity in a person. It is expressed by the optative component [of the verbal suffix]. For, one necessarily understands 'this induces me to act, since it entails an activity conducive to my undertaking of an activity' when one hears an optative ending.[16]

But those primers have an overall different agenda (practical and not theoretical), since they aim at presenting a clear overlook of the system and not at a critical investigation of its tenets, and are by and large not written for philosophical purposes. Thus, they cannot be a viable option for a cross-philosophical enterprise.

Jayanta Bhaṭṭa on Exhortation

This leads us back to the priority-question we started with: Which texts shall we start reading/studying, in order to understand Indian sentence-theories and re-think linguistic studies along them?

The present author's answer is to suggest Jayanta Bhaṭṭa's Nyāyamañjarī.[17]

Jayanta lived during the reign of the king Śaṅkaravarman (883-902, dates based on the *Rājataraṇginī*, see Stein 1961, p. 98) in Kaśmīr. He was a Naiyāyika (i.e., an adherent of the Nyāya school) and the Nyāyamañjarī is his opus magnum. This is an encyclopedic work dealing with instruments of knowledge (*pramāṇas*) and objects to be known (*prameyas*). Four books out of twelve are dedicated to language (which is included in the first group).

How can Jayanta be an answer to the problems sketched above?

- Because of historical advantages: Jayanta is earlier than many insiders (see Kataoka 2008, pp. 210-209, which explains how Jayanta offers in many cases the first extant interpretation of Kumārila) and definitely much earlier than all primers (which have been written only after the XV c.).
- Because he is himself a mediator (not an insider): Jayanta is indeed a Naiyāyika who knows a lot about Mīmāṃsā, but writes for a Naiyāyika public: Hence, he needs to explain the theories he deals with.
- Because he is a philosopher: Unlike the authors of primers, who are mainly concerned with giving an overall view of the whole system, Jayanta pauses on each topic and discusses it thoroughly.
- Because he writes in order to understand: As it is immediately evident out of the very bulkiness of the part of NM 5 dedicated to *śabdabhāvanā*, Jayanta carefully examines each definition rather than presupposing them.
- Because he is reliable in depicting his opponents' views: He is fair against opponents and his philosophical attitude does not make him interpret freely his predecessors' opinions, as it is often the case with other commentators who are either biased against a certain view, or more philosophically creative, such as Prajñākaragupta or Someśvara Bhaṭṭa. Such commentators end up being less reliable because they integrate what is not found in the original theories, develop them further, emend them, etc.

Jayanta on *śabdabhāvanā*

The discussion on *śabdabhāvanā* is found in NM 5, after (a) a discussion on what is the meaning of linguistic elements (śabda), and (b) a discussion on the nature of action (bhāvanā). Thus, Jayanta arrives at *śabdabhāvanā* because of the strength of the arguments he is dealing with. By contrast, in other texts, this and similar topics are dealt with in accordance with their place in the text they comment upon or in accordance with ritual purposes (e.g., the MNP and the AS do not deal with the restrictive prescription *niyamavidhi* while discussing the nature of exhortation, but rather while discussing the role of mantras within the Vedic ritual[18]). In other words, Jayanta is led by theoretical concerns.

Jayanta's definition of *śabdabhāvanā* runs as follows:

> The linguistic force is that function pertaining to language which causes people to undertake actions and in which the undertaking of the activity reaches the status of something to be done.[19]

The chief elements of this definitions are that the *śabdabhāvanā* is a function (*vyāpara*), related to language (*śabdagata*) and inherently prescriptive (*sādhyatāṃ pratipadyate*).

Jayanta on "To whom does the illocutionary force belong?"

This leads us back to the question mentioned above ((1), p.6), namely, "to whom does the illocutionary force belong?" In other words, "is language by itself able to convey a perlocutionary effect or does it depend on its listeners in order to do it?" In Jayanta's terminology, the first question can be specified as "How can the burden of expressing the illocutionary force rest on a function?"

Jayanta addresses the problem insofar as he investigates on the relation between exhortation and prescriptive verbal endings. Do prescriptive verbal endings directly induce one to act, or is it their functioning (*vyāpāra*), which induces one to act? The alternative reproduces the gist of question (1).

If exhortative verbal endings would in themselves express the exhortation, then everyone —just by hearing them— would undertake an activity. Even young children or strangers, who do not understand Sanskrit, would be induced to act by the force of exhortative endings, if this were intrinsic in them and did not depend on their function. Moreover, the relation between the exhortative endings and exhortation itself would be twofold, insofar as exhortation would be their product, i.e., it would not exist before them, but also their meaning. And how could a semanteme mean something which it itself produces just by the fact of being uttered? [20]

If, by contrast, one maintains that the exhortation is conveyed by a function of the exhortative endings, then the theory amounts to the following scheme:

exhortative endings

↓

exhortative endings' function, i.e., conveying a meaning

↓

comprehension of this meaning by the listener

↓

effect on the listener: exhortation

In this way, the intermediate step of understanding the exhortative endings' meaning is added. Hence, the burden of the illocutionary force is carried by both language and its listeners, who cooperate to the exhortation insofar as they must be proficient in language use in general and have understood the specific meaning at stake. In other words, Jayanta's answer to question (1) is that language is a vehicle of illocutionary force not in itself, as if it had a magical power, but rather insofar as it conveys a meaning. The illocutionary force depends, thus, on the meaning conveyed by a certain statement and not on its sheer utterance. The illocutionary force, consequently, does not depend on the phonic aspect of language, but on the pieces of knowledge it conveys. It is, hence, rooted in the epistemological aspect of language as instrument for conveying knowledge.

Indeed, Jayanta (like all other *vākyaśāstra*vādins, but in a clearer way) links what we would call linguistics and epistemology.

Linguistics and epistemology

Non-descriptive (in Austin's terminology: "non-constative") statements have been also in Speech Act theory a chance to re-consider epistemological issues. Consider, for instance, Austin's discussion of "false promises" in his first lecture:

> In the particular case of promising, as with many other performatives, it is appropriate that the person uttering the promise should have a certain intention, viz. here to keep his word: and perhaps of all concomitants this looks the most suitable to be that which 'I promise' does describe or record. Do we not actually, when such intention is absent, speak

> of a 'false' promise? Yet so to speak is *not* to say that the utterance 'I promise that...' is false, in the sense that though he states that he does, he doesn't, or that though he describes he misdescribes —misreports. For he *does* promise: the promise here is not even *void*, though it is given *in bad faith*. His utterance is perhaps misleading, probably deceitful and doubtless wrong, but it is not a lie or a misstatement. At most we might make out a case for saying that it implies or insinuates a falsehoods or a misstatement (to the effect that he does not intend to do something): but that is a very different matter. Moreover, we do not speak of a false bet or a false christening; and that we *do* speak of a false promise need commit us no more than the fact that we speak of a false move. 'False' is not necessarily used of statements only (Austin 1975, p. 11).

In the second lecture, Austin defines "performative utterances":

> These have on the face of them the look —or at least the grammatical make-up— of 'statements'; but nevertheless they are seen, when more closely inspected, to be, quite plainly, not utterances which could be 'true' or 'false'. Yet to be 'true' or 'false' is traditionally the characteristic mark of a statement (Austin 1975, p. 12).

In other words, Austin's answer seems to be that illocutionary speech acts show that truth-values cannot be applied to all sorts of utterances, but rather only to the sub-set of constative utterances. On the contrary, when a performative utterance has, e.g., not been performed by the appropriate person (for instance when someone who is not in charge of it pretends to baptize a ship), or, e.g., is not followed by the appropriate action (for instance when one does not actually give something after having said "I give this to you"), Austin speaks (see Austin 1975, p. 15) of "unhappy" performative utterances. Further, he distinguishes the two cases labelling the first ones as "abuses" and the last ones as "misfires" (when the act is not accomplished at all).[21]

More generally, Austin's point is that illocutionary speech acts are just acts. And, like any other act, they can fail to attain their result or be miscarried (Austin 1975, p. 18). His analysis, hence, plays down the linguistic specificity of Speech Acts. Consider, for instance, Austin's insistence on the equivalence of the linguistic and the non-linguistic version of the same act:

> [I]nfelicity is an ill to which all acts are heir which have the general character of ritual or ceremonial. [...] This is clear if only from the mere fact that many conventional acts, such as betting or conveyance of property, can be performed in non-verbal ways (Austin 1975, p. 19).

To sum up, Austin stresses the nature of acts of speech acts and, hence, bans them out of epistemology.[22]

A study by a scholar of Indian philosophy, Arnold 2001, compares Austin and the Buddhist author Candrakīrti, primarily focusing on their epistemologies and on how they are linked to ordinary language. Interestingly, hence, Dan Arnold also uses the Speech Act theory in order to reframe epistemology in a way which avoids the strict commitment to certainty typical of contemporary epistemology in the West.[23]

Jayanta on linguistics and epistemology

Austin stresses the nature of acts of speech acts and, consequently, excludes any epistemological role for them. By contrast, Jayanta and many other Indian thinkers tend to reframe epistemology in order for it to include also directive speech acts.

In this regard, one might ask:

> What is the meaning of a prescription? In epistemological terms, how is its truth-value to be analysed? (2)

A first, tempting solution might be to rephrase a prescription in terms more easily manageable by epistemology, i.e., in descriptive terms. A prescription, maintains for instance Maṇḍana Miśra, is nothing but a statement conveying the fact that the action to be undertaken is a means towards something desired. If this were the case, it would then be easier to determine its truth value. If, for instance, one says "The one who desires to be fat should drink cream,"[24] it is easy to determine that, in fact, cream is full of fats and that it is, hence, the suitable instrument for the purpose of becoming fatter.

According to all other *Mīmāṃsakas*, including Jayanta, however, a prescription does not convey the idea that an action is the instrument for a certain result. It rather conveys the relation of thing to be done and instrument to achieve it (*sādhya-sādhana-bhāva*) holding between the two. Hence, it cannot be rephrased as a description.

The rephrasing solution is, indeed, appealing, but it violates the specificity of exhortative sentences against descriptive ones. There is indeed a difference between

"Cream is the means to become fatter" and "Drink cream!" as shown by the fact that the two sentences can be used together and the second one is not perceived as redundant ("Cream is the means to become fatter, hence, if you want to increase your weight, drink cream!").

Since the descriptive paraphrase fails to be an accurate reproduction of an exhortation, we could consider question (2) also from the point of view of what we would call pragmatics. Does a prescription have just a pragmatic output, i.e., the arousal of one's intention/desire to undertake the action enjoined? In this case, the truth-value of a prescription could only be pragmatically determined. In Austin's terminology, it would be recognized through its perlocutionary effect. In other words, a prescription which does not have any perlocutionary effect could be said to be false. A connected question sounds as follows: is a prescription which has no authority at all over us still a prescription? If it is not, then, an exhortation would depend only on its perlocutionary effects. For instance, does a prescription about the way meat should be cooked read by a vegetarian reader of a book on the anthropology of cooking styles still retain its exhortative value?

The answer depends on how one defines a prescription (i.e., if formally or pragmatically). I am inclined to think that, according to the Mīmāṃsā analysis, it would no longer be an exhortation, because a prescription needs desire for its result on the part of its listener (see Freschi 2007 and Freschi 2012). In the case of a slave being directed to carry something, the desire could be rephrased as her desire to satisfy her master, or to avoid a punishment, but the role of desire cannot be ruled out altogether. Hence, exhortation is not thought of as a purely linguistic phenomenon, independent of whoever listens to it. There is a link to pragmatics, via the definition of a context, of suitable listeners, and of the range of authority of the utterance (in the Speech Act Theory, which focuses on the speaker, this would be tantamount to the range of authority of the speaker). In other words, the listener is part of the process through which a statement displays its exhortative meaning.

On the other hand, a prescription induces one to act insofar as it conveys a meaning ("a prescription causes to act only if joined to [its meaning's] cognition" *vidhis tu sapratyayasya eva pravartakaḥ*, VV, p. 65).

Therefore:

listener's desire ↘ exhortation ↙ exhortative meaning

Hence, a prescription has not just a pragmatic aspect. Rather, its pragmatic consequences are caused at least also by its epistemological outputs (i.e., its meaning) and Jayanta clearly states the precedence of the latter over the former, insofar as the discussions about language are part of the broader topic of epistemology. This, by the way, also means that epistemology in India is a broader field than its Western counterpart (which tends to be tantamount to a philosophy of exact sciences). It can accommodate within itself all sorts of cognition (it also includes long debates on doubtful or erroneous cognitions) and not only descriptive ones (see Freschi 2010). It is from this point of view that a question such as (2) does not appear meaningless.

Thus, Jayanta stresses the epistemological aspect of exhortations. From this point of view he is closer to

Searle's claim (against Austin) that the illocutionary force is an aspect of meaning (see Sbisà 2009, p. 234).

An exhortation, writes Jayanta (GS p. 65) does not induce people to act like the wind forces them to move, that is, automatically. One only acts insofar as one has understood the prescription. Hence, an intermediate epistemological stage is unavoidable. This does not only require competence in language use, but also adherence to the world-view presupposed by the prescription. A Sanskritist may now object that no Indian author would accept that the Vedas might be thought as not prescriptive. There is indeed a subtle boundary between what is ontologically not a prescription and what just does not *function* subjectively like one. In general, I am inclined to think that a *vākyaśāstra*-author would say that the Vedas do not cease to be prescriptive, because they address people who desire happiness, and everyone desires happiness. But I never found an explicit argument for it in the texts I am aware of.

To summarize: A prescription does not exist in an epistemological vacuum. It induces to act—via its meaning—suitable listeners, who must long for its outcome.

Jayanta's is a double approach, with epistemological concern overtopping the pragmatical one, which is still present through desire. In Austin's terminology, one could say that Jayanta's analysis of exhortations takes into account perlocution and language-based illocutionary force.

Conclusions

Exhortation from both Indian and Western perspectives:

The Indian sentence-linguistics (*vākyaśāstra*) is usually neglected, but significant, also insofar as it addresses problems from a perspective different from the ones common in mainstream linguistics. Conversely, Western linguistics can spread light on aspects of Indian thought by making one reflect on them from a different point of view.[25]

For instance, exhortation can be analyzed from the point of view of the speaker, of the listener and of language itself and the *vākyaśāstra* may co-operate with the Speech Act theory to highlight also the latter two aspects (whereas Searle only stressed the role of the speaker).

Furthermore, exhortation can be dealt with as a linguistic phenomenon (as in Western mainstream linguistics, which considers it only an exception to descriptive statements), or from the point of view of its pragmatic outputs (as in Austin), or as primarily an epistemological phenomenon (as in mainstream Indian thought). The *vākyaśāstra* may show how linguistics can be seen within an enlarged epistemology, with pragmatics as part of the context.

Finally, what is the role of the meaning? Austin seems to rather stress what a speaker does or effects on a listener through his speech act. By contrast, *vākyaśāstra* authors agree with Searle that the illocutionary force is part of the meaning and is not situated outside it.

Linguistics: Indian Sources

Taking into account Indian sources means broadening one's perspective, opening it to new questions and to a highly developed discipline offering insightful answers. However, in order to approach it, one has to carefully select her textual tools.

One can count on a solid tradition of studies for Indian Grammar and—though in a minor degree—for the Buddhist approach to language. The *Mīmāṃsā* approach is, by contrast, still less known and one needs to count on Sanskrit sources with little help from secondary literature. In this article it has been shown that a good starting point is Jayanta Bhaṭṭa's NM 5. Jayanta has the uncommon advantage of being a philosopher and being able to make his argument clearly; he can thus spread light on other authors.

Abbreviations

A: Brahmamitra Avasthi, ed. (1978). *The Vākyārthamātṛkā of Śālikanātha with Hindī commentary*. Dillī: Indu Prakāśana.

MK: Kevālanandasarasvatī, ed. (1952-1954). *Mīmāṃsākośa. Vol. 7 vols. Prājñapāṭhaśālāmaṇḍala Granthamālā*. Wai: Prājñapāṭhaśālā.

MNS: Mahādeva Vedāntin (2010). *Mīmāṃsānyāyasaṅgraha. A Compendium on the Principles of Mīmāṃsā*, edited and translated by James Benson. Ed. by James Benson. Wiesbaden: Harrassowitz.

MS, ŚBh, TV: Kashinath Vasudev Abhyankar and Ganesasastri Am-badasa Jośī, eds. (1971–1980). *Śrīmajjaiminipraṇite Mīmāṃsādarśane: Mīmāṃsaka-kaṇṭhīrava-Kumārilabhaṭṭapraṇita-Tantravārtikasahita-Śābarabhāṣyopetaḥ*. 2nd (1st ed. 1929-1934). Ānandāśramasaṃskṛtagranthāvaliḥ 97. Poona: Anandasrama.

NM: K. S. Varadācārya, ed. (1969, 1983). *Nyāyamañjarī of Jayanta Bhaṭṭa with Ṭippani—Nyāyasaurabha by the Editor. Vol. 2*. Mysore: Oriental Research Institute.

VV: Maṇḍana Miśra and Vācaspati Miśra (1978). *Vidhiviveka of Śrī Maṇḍana Miśra with the commentary Nyāyakaṇikā of Vācaspati Miśra*. Ed. by Mahāprabhulāla Gosvāmī. Vārāṇasī: Tara Publications.

Notes

1. I am grateful to Artemij Keidan and Alberto Todeschini for their comments on an earlier draft of this paper.

2. For an accurate, insightful and thought-provoking appraisal of the *Nirukta,* of its implicit strategies and of its impact, see Kahrs 1998. Kahrs' main thesis (summarized in Kahrs 1984) has been criticized in Scharf 2001.

3. On the Buddhist epistemological approach to language, namely the *apoha* theory, a summary of the philosophical issues at stake is Siderits, Tillemans, and Chakrabarti 2011, and one more oriented to the texts is Krasser and McAllister 2013. Although I am not aware of anything similar dedicated to the Nyāya approach to language, several excellent scholars of Nyāya have focused also on its linguistic theories. See, for instance, Ganeri 1999 and Matilal 1990.

4. Most of the few exceptions are due to scholars focusing primarily on Nyāya, and who have reached Mīmāṃsā through it. Examples of this include Sen 2005, and Matilal and Sen 1988. Similarly, starting from a different perspective, but also not from Mīmāṃsā, there are Siderits 1985, Siderits 1986, and Raja 1994. Then there are some excellences of the past, such as Edgerton 1928 and Rāmasvāmiśāstrī 1952, who, unfortunately, have not been enough to pave the way for further systematic studies. D'Sa 1980 is thought-provoking, but often too interpretative. Studies written from an inner-Indian point of view (such as the ones included in Joshi 1980) might be good, but are of little use for linguists, since they tend not to address the problems of the Sanskrit texts they analyze from a philosophical or linguistic perspective, but rather to reproduce them. Worth mentioning because of their philosophical depth are also, without aiming at being

exhaustive, the short, but clear Chakrabarti 1989, the insightful Taber 1989, Bilimoria 1994, and the portions dedicated to Mīmāṃsā in Bilimoria 1988.

5. "Exactly so in common usage (*loka*) does proficient learning (*vyutpatti*) occur for the first time. The elder senior employs (*prayuj-*) the sentence 'Devadatta, bring the cow!' Thereafter, the middle senior undertakes the [corresponding] activity (*pravṛt-*). Then, one who is not concerned with this activity (*taṭastha*) and who desires to learn the language (*vyutpitsu*), thinks: 'His undertaking of an activity (*pravṛtti*) presupposes (*pūrvikā*) a cognition, because it is an undertaking, like my undertakings too. And this cognition was born from a sentence, since it came immediately after it.' The proficient learning (*vyutpatti*) of the sentence-meaning of the sentence was initially mixed (*sammuh-*) [because one knew the total meaning of the sentence, but not of its words]. [But,] by seeing again and again in this way the use (*prayoga*), [finally the proficient learning] that the meaning of that sentence is the bringing of the cow, arises.

"After that, having sometimes been employed, the sentence 'Bring the horse!' and having followed the corresponding activity (*pravṛtti*), one notices the addition (*āvāpa*) of the word (*pada*) 'horse' and the connection (*anvaya*) of that meant entity, and the removal (*udvāpa*) of the word 'cow' and the non-connection (*ananvaya*) of that meant entity [within the injunctive sentence]. Therefore, through addition and removal the proficient learning (*vyutpatti*) of every [word-meaning] comes about, of the word 'horse' for the meant entity *equus caballus* (*haya*) as related to other meant entities and of the word 'cow' for the meant entity having a dewlap etc., similarly [related to other meant entities]. (*itthaṃ tāvat prathamaṃ loke vyutpattiprakāraḥ, –uttamavṛddhas tāvat "devadatta gām ānaya" iti vākyaṃ prayuṅkte. tadanu madhyamavṛddhaḥ pravartate. tadānīṃ taṭastho vyutpitsur evaṃ manyate —asya pravṛttir jñānapūrvikā, pravṛttitvāt, madīyapravṛttivat. tac ca jñānaṃ vākyajanyaṃ, tadanantarabhāvitvād iti. itthaṃ bhūyobhūyaḥ prayogadarśanena prathamaṃ tāvad vākyasya vākyārthe sammugdhā vyutpattir jāyate asya vākyasya gavānayanam artha iti. paścāt kadācit "aśvam ānaya" iti vākyaprayoge tathaiva pravṛttau aśvapadāvāpe tadarthānvayād gopadodvāpe tadarthānanvayād āvāpodvāpābhyām aśvapadasyārthāntarānvite hayārthe gopadasya ca tādṛśe sāsnādimadarthe pratyekaṃ vyutpattir jāyate. TR III 5.2.1).* The same process is also described in several other *Mīmāṃsā* texts, for instance, PrP, *vākyārthamātṛkā* I, ad 6, A, p. 35, Sarma 1990, p. 4; PrP, *vākyārthamātṛkā* II ad 3-4ab, p. 30 and PrP, *vākyārthamātṛkā* II ad 9, p. 38; *Nyāyaratnamālā, vidhinirṇaya* ad 1, p. 40.

6. Austin also stresses the importance of the context, though understanding it in a pragmatic sense: "Speaking generally, it is always necessary that the circumstances in which the words are uttered should be in some way, or ways, appropriate, and it is very commonly necessary that either the speaker himself or other persons should also perform certain other actions, whether 'physical' or 'mental' actions or even acts of uttering further words" (Austin 1975, p. 8).

7. "It was for too long the assumption of philosophers that the business of a 'statement' can only be to 'describe' some state of affairs, or to 'state some fact', which it must do either truly or falsely" (Austin 1975, p. 1). See also, to list only some random examples, Lyons 1968, Simone 1996, Devitt and Hanley 2006, and most other companions and textbooks on linguistics

8. "Phatic" refers to the usage of language for social interactions rather than for asking questions or conveying information, e.g., "Hello!" If one utters a pheme (i.e., a phone which conforms to the lexical and

grammatical rules of a given language) with a more or less definite sense and reference, one is also uttering a rheme, and, thus, performing a "rhetic" act. Rhemes are a sub-class of phemes, which in turn are a sub-class of phones (the latter term encompasses all sorts of utterances, even if grammatically unsound and therefore not understandable). One cannot perform a rheme without also performing a pheme and a phone. The performance of these three acts is the performance of a locution.

9. Sbisà 2009, p. 233.

10. A related question, in purely Speech-Act terminology, is Sbisà's in the following passage: "Are illocutionary forces understood by virtue of the semantics of their linguistic indicators or by means of pragmatically invited inferences? Illocutionary force occupies an ambiguous position between semantics and pragmatics. It could be considered as a purely semantic phenomenon, wholly dependent on the codified meaning of words [1], only if it were possible to assign illocutionary forces to speech acts on the sole basis of the linguistic indicating device (or set of indicating devices). But this is not the case. [...] Is then illocutionary force wholly pragmatic [2]? This solution would involve a minimization of the contribution of linguistic illocutionary indicators to the understanding of illocutionary force" (Sbisà 2009, p. 237). Indian *vākyaśāstra* authors would stress sentence-meaning over word-meanings in option [1].

11. Again, one is reminded of Siderits, Tillemans, and Chakrabarti 2011 and Matilal and Sen 1988 for instances of this approach.

12. *śabdabhāvanā tu liṅtvena vācyā māṃ pravartayati veda ity anubhavasiddhā* (*MNS* 2.1.1). The translation is James Benson's.

13. For instance: "The linguistic *bhāvanā* is called like that because of the function of language" (*śabdabhāvanā*

iti śabdavyāpāratvād ucyate, Gāgābhaṭṭa 1933 (repr.) p. 90); "The linguistic *bhāvanā*, obtained only through the suffixes of optative, imperative, subjunctive and gerundive, is understood through the optative, etc." (*śabdabhāvanā liṅleṭloṭtavyapratyayamātragatā liṅādibhir gamyate, Jaiminīyanyāyamālāvistara* 2.1.1, varṇaka 2); "That function of language in regard to the arousal of a cognition is called with the word '*śabdabhāvanā*.' The word causes to act insofar as it causes such a cognition to rise, not insofar as it declares indifferency (*Nyāya-sudhā*, p. 57, qtd. in MK, s.v. I am not sure about this translation).

14. A Mīmāṃsaka who lived between Kumārila and Jayanta.

15. *sa khalu śabdabhedo vā, tadvyāpārātiśayo vā, arthabhedo vā. yadabhidhānāc chabdo 'pi tathā vyap-adeśyaḥ*. The following verse, excluding the first alternative is more obscure: *pramāṇatvād aniyamāt pravṛtteḥ saṃvidāśrayāt | samabhivyāhṛteḥ śabdo na vidhiḥ kāryakalpanāt ||*

16. *puruṣapravṛttyanukūlo bhāvayitur vyāpāraviśeṣaḥ śābdī bhāvanā. sā ca liṅaṃśenocyate. liṅśravaṇe 'yam māṃ pravartayati matpravṛttyanukūlavyāpāravān ayam iti niyamena pratīteḥ* (*AS* 1.6).

17. The *NM* still awaits a complete critical edition. Apart from the editio princeps, Jayanta Bhaṭṭa 1895-1896, I will use in the following the text edited in *NM*.

18. Mantras are useful, according to Mīmāṃsakas, insofar as they remind one of the ritual elements he has to use. Since, however, other instruments could be used for the same purpose (a written list, a suitable arrangement of the ritual elements on a table, etc.), it is explained that mantras alone have to be used for this purpose, due to a restrictive prescription (*MNP* 239–241).

19. *yas tu śabdagataḥ prayojakavyāpāro yatra pu-ruṣapravṛttiḥ sādhyatāṃ pratipadyate sā śabdabhāvanā*

(*NM* 5, Jayanta Bhaṭṭa 1895-1896, p. 67; *NM*, p. 97). I am grateful to Alessandro Graheli for having discussed with me parallel instances of the usage of pratipadyate in the *NM*. As for the problem, mentioned-above, of the meaning of the compound "*śabdabhāvanā*," it might be interesting to note that Jayanta seems to favor a karmadhāraya interpretation of the compound.

20. This case is quite different from that of a performative speech act such as "I promise," which produces the effect it describes, since such a speech act needs to be understood—and not just uttered—in order to produce its effect. Hence, the performative character is achieved via its meaning.

21. A more comprehensive scheme can be found in Austin 1975, p. 18.

22. M. Sbisà writes: "The context-bound nature of speech acts (including assertions) is widely acknowledged, but challenges to the role of truth conditions with respect to content are refrained from" (Sbisà 2009, p. 242).

23. "Thus, our comparison of Austin and Candrakīrti has, I think, both elucidated Candrakīrti's often elliptical argument and helped to clarify the extent to which Austin's project is in fact rather closely related to his writings on epistemology and in particular to a critique of the kind of radical skepticism to which Austin takes traditional epistemology to be a response" (Arnold 2001, p. 267). I am indebted to Alberto Todeschini who pointed out this study.

24. This example is found in Mīmāṃsā texts, e.g. *TR* IV 9.3.1.

25. Another instance of the fruitful interaction between Speech Act theory and Indian linguistics is Todeschini 2010, where the author discusses the rules of debate listed in the *Nyāyasūtra* in the light of Grice's "Cooperative Principle." It is not by chance that such a

comparison finds place, again, within the wider framework of a textual context (here: of a debate). I hope that Todeschini will elaborate further on the structural reasons of the parallel he highlighted.

Works Cited

Abhyankar, Kashinath Vasudev and Ganesasastri Ambadasa Jośī, eds. *Śrīmajjaiminipraṇite Mīmāṃsādarśane: Mīmāṃsākakanthirava-Kumārilabhaṭṭapraṇita-Tantravārtikasahita-Śābarabhāsyopetaḥ*. 2nd (1st ed. 1929-1934). *Ānandāśramasaṃskṛtagranthāvaliḥ* 97. Poona: Anandasrama. 1971-1980.

Alfieri, Luca. "A Contribution to the History of the Concept of Root." *Proceedings of "The Study of South Asia between Antiquity and Modernity: Coffee Break Conference 2."* Eds. Marco Ferrante and Artemij Keidan. (forthcoming).

Arnold, Dan. "How to Do Things with Candrakīrti: A Comparative Study in Anti-Skepticism." *Philosophy East and West* 51.2 (April 2001): 247-279.

Austin, John Langshaw. *How to Do Things with Words.* 2nd ed. Oxford: Clarendon Press, 1975.

Avasthi, Brahmamitra, ed. *The Vākyārthamātṛkā of Śālikanātha with Hindī Commentary*. Dillī: Indu Prakāśana, 1978.

Bach, Kent. "Speech Acts and Pragmatics." *The Blackwell Guide to the Philosophy of Language.* Eds. Michael Devitt and Richard Hanley. Oxford: Blackwell, 2006. pp. 147-167.

Bilimoria, Puruṣottama. *Śabdapramāṇa, Word and Knowledge: a Doctrine in Mimamsa-Nyaya Philosophy (with Reference to Advaita Vedānta-paribhāṣā "Āgama") Towards a Framework for Śruti-prāmāṇya.* Boston: Kluwer Academic, 1988.

———. "Autpattika: The 'Originary' Signifier-Signified

Relation in Mīmāṃsā and Deconstructive Semiology." *Studies in Mīmāṃsā. Dr. Mandan Mishra Felicitation Volume*. Ed. R.C. Dwivedi. Delhi: Motilal Banarsidass, 1994. pp. 187-205.

Chakrabarti, Arindam. "Sentence-Holism, Context-Principle and Connected-Designation Anvitābhidhāna: Three Doctrines or One?" *Journal of Indian Philosophy* 17.1 (1989): 37-41.

Copi, Irving M. and Carl Cohen. *Introduction to Logic*. Upper Saddle River, NJ: Pearson, 1986.

Devitt, Michael and Richard Hanley, eds. *The Blackwell Guide to the Philosophy of Language*. Oxford: Blackwell, 2006..

D'Sa, Francis Xavier. *Śabdaprāmāṇyam in Śabara and Kumārila: Towards a Study of the Mīmāṃsā Experience of Language*. Vienna: De Nobili Research Library, 1980.

Edgerton, Franklin (1928). "Some Linguistics Notes on the Mīmāṅsā [sic] System." *Language* 4 (1928): 171-177.

Freschi, Elisa. "*Desidero Ergo Sum*: The Subject as the Desirous One in Mīmāṃsā." *Rivista degli Studi Orientali* 80.1 (2007): 51-61.

———. "Facing the Boundaries of Epistemology: Kumārila on Error and Negative Cognition." *Journal of Indian Philosophy* 38 (2010): 39-48.

———. "Action, Desire and Subjectivity in Prābhākara Mīmāṃsā." *Hindu and Buddhist Ideas in Dialogue: Self and No-Self*. Eds. Irina Kuznetsova, Jonardon Ganeri and Chakravarti Ram-Prasad. Farnham, Surrey, England: Ashgate, 2012. pp. 147-164.

Gāgābhaṭṭa. *Bhāṭṭacintāmaṇi*. Ed. Sūryanārāyaṇa Śarmaśukla. Chowkhamba Sanskrit Series 25 and 27. Benares: Vidya Vilas Press, 1933.

Ganeri, Jonardon. *Semantic Powers: Meaning and the Means of Knowing in Classical Indian Philosophy*. Oxford; NY: Oxford UP, 1999.

Jayanta Bhaṭṭa. *The Nyāyamañjarī of Jayanta Bhaṭṭa*. Ed. Gaṅgādhara Śāstrī Tailaṅga. Vizianagaram Sanskrit Series 10. Benares: E.J. Lazarus, 1895-1896.

Joshi, Shivram Dattatray, ed. *Proceedings of the Winter Institute on Ancient Indian Theories on Sentence-Meaning*. Publications of the Centre of Advanced Study in Sanskrit 6. Poona: U of Poona P, 1980.

Kahrs, Eivind. "Yāska's Nirukta: The Quest for a New Interpretation." *Indologica Taurinensia* 12 (1984): 139-154.

———. *Indian Semantic Analysis: The Nirvacana Tradition*. NY: Cambridge UP, 1998.

Kataoka, Kei. "A Critical Edition of Bhaṭṭa Jayanta's *Nyāyamañjarī*: The Section on Kumārila's Refutation of the Apoha Theory." *Minutes of the Institute of Oriental Culture, University of Tokyo* 154 (2008): 182-212.

Keidan, Artemij (2011). "The Kāraka-Vibhakti Device as a Heuristic Tool for the Compositional History of Pāṇini's Aṣṭādhyāyī." *Rivista degli Studi Orientali, Proceedings of "The Study of Asia Between Antiquity and Modernity: Coffee Break Conference 3."* Eds. Elisa Freschi, et al. 84.1 (2012): 273-288.

Krasser, Helmut and Patrick Mc Allister, eds. *Proceedings of the Apoha Workshop, 16-20 April 2012*. Wien: Österreichische Akademie der Wissenschaften, 2013.

Kunjunni Raja, Kumarapuram. "Mīmāṃsā Views on Sentence-Meaning: Some Problems." *Studies in Mīmāṃsā. Dr. Mandan Mishra Felicitation Volume*. Ed. R.C. Dwivedi. Delhi: Motilal Banarsidass, 1994, pp. 207-214.

Lyons, John. *Introduction to Theoretical Linguistics*. London: Cambridge UP, 1968.

Mahādeva Vedāntin. *Mīmāṃsānyāyasaṅgraha. A Compendium on the Principles of Mīmāṃsā, edited and translated by James Benson*. Ed. James Benson. Wiesbaden: Harrassowitz, 2010.

Maṇḍana Miśra and Vācaspati Miśra. *Vidhiviveka of Śrī Maṇḍana Miśra with the Commentary Nyāyakaṇikā of Vācaspati Miśra*. Ed. Mahāprabhulāla Gosvāmī. Vārāṇasī: Tara Publications, 1978.

Matilal, Bimal Krishna. *The Word and the World: India's Contribution to the Study of Language*. NY: Oxford UP, 1990.

Matilal, Bimal Krishna and Prabal Kumar Sen (1988). "The Context Principle and Some Indian Controversies Over Meaning." *Mind* 97.385 (January 1988): 73-97.

McCrea, Lawrence. "Desecularization in Indian Intellectual Culture, 900–1300 AD." (forthcoming).

Rāmasvāmiśāstrī, V.A. "Bhāvanā, the Leading Concept of Verbal Cognition." *Bhāratīya Vidyā* 13 (1952): 25-32.

Sarasvati, Kevalānanda, ed. *Mīmāṃsākoṣa*. 7 vols. Wai: Prājña Pāṭhaśālā Maṇḍala, 1952-1954.

Sarma, Rajendra Nath. *Verbal Knowledge in Prābhākara Mīmāṃsā. Including the Text of Śālikanātha Miśra's Vākyārthamātṛkā*. Sri Garib Das Oriental Series 60. Delhi: Sri Satguru, 1990.

Sbisà, Marina. "Speech Act Theory." *Key Notions for Pragmatics*. Eds. Jef Verschueren and Jan-Ola Östman. Amsterdam: John Benjamins Publishing Company, 2009: pp. 229-243.

Scharf, Peter M. "Review of Eivind Kahrs' *Indian Semantic Analysis: the 'Nirvacana' Tradition*." *Journal of the American Oriental Society* 121.1 (2001): 116-120.

Searle, J.R. *Speech Acts: An Essay in the Philosophy of Language*. Cambrdige: Cambridge UP, 1969.

Sen, Prabal Kumar. "Nyāya Criticism of *Anvitābhidhānavāda* and *Abhihitānvayavāda*." *Language and Communication. A Philosophical Study*. Rabindra Bharati Readings in Philosophy. Volume One. Eds. Sandhya Basu and Madhucchanda Sen. Kolkata:

Rabindra Bharati University, 2005. pp. 51-81.
Siderits, Mark. "The Prābhākara Mīmāṃsā Theory of Related Designation." *Analytical Philosophy in Comparative Perspective*. Eds. Bimal Kriṣṇa Matilal and J. L. Shaw. Dordrecht: Reidel, 1985. pp. 253-297.
———. "The Sense-Reference Distinction in Indian Philosophy of Language." *Synthese* 69 (1986): 81-106.
Siderits, Mark, Tom J. F. Tillemans, and Arindam Chakrabarti, eds. *Apoha: Buddhist Nominalism and Human Cognition.* NY: Columbia UP, 2011.
Simone, Raffaele. *Fondamenti di Linguistica*. Bari: Laterza, 1996.
Squarcini, Federico, ed. *Verso l'India, Oltre l'India: Scritti e Ricerche sulle Tradizioni Intellettuali Sudasiatiche.* Milano: Memesis, 2002.
Stein, M. Aurel, ed. *Kalhaṇa's Rājataraṅginī. A Chronicle of the Kings of Kaśmīr. Translated with an Introduction, Commentary & Appendices*. 2nd ed. Delhi: Motilal Banarsidass, 1961.
Taber, John. "The Theory of the Sentence in Pūrva Mīmāṃsā and Western Philosophy." *Journal of Indian Philosophy* 17.4 (1989): 407-430.
Todeschini, Alberto. "Twenty-Two Ways to Lose a Debate: A Gricean Look at the Nyāyasūtra's Point of Defeat." *Journal of Indian Philosophy* 38.1 (2010): 49-74.
Varadācārya, K. S., ed. *Nyāyamañjarī of Jayanta Bhaṭṭa with Ṭippani—Nyāyasaurabha by the Editor*. Mysore: Oriental Research Institute, 1969.

Dr. Elisa Freschi is Project leader of the Lise Meitner project "Epistemology of Sacred Texts in the Sesvaramimamsa," hosted at the Austrian Academy of Sciences, IKGA, Vienna.

CHAPTER 4

ARTEM KOBZEV & VICTORIA LYSENKO

Was there a Chinese Form of Atomism? The Vaiṣeśika Atomistic Text in the Chinese Philosophical Tradition

India and China are deeply separated by many factors: by their language, culture, history, thought. This underlying difference between them makes them ideal subjects for the cross-cultural studies, especially for investigation into the mechanisms of assimilation of one cultural paradigm in terms of another. However, this richest resource is used very rarely and insufficiently. We would like to propose a Sino-indological project which will be based on the study of one of the earliest texts of the Indian traditional philosophical school Vaiṣeśika, that came to our time only in the Chinese translation. This text is called in Sanskrit *Daśapadārthaśāstra* ("Science of the ten categories"), the full name being *Vaiṣeśika-nikāya-daśa-padārtha-śāstra* (Chinese, *Sheng-zong shi ju-yi lun* - "Shastra / Judgments on the Ten Categories of Vaiṣeśika / School of Winning [Opinions]"). Its author, Candramati (Chinese, *Hui-yue*), supposedly lived in the 5th century C.E.

The text was brought to China and translated in 648 by the famous Chinese Buddhist pilgrim Xuan-zang. We may suppose that the *Daśapadārthaśāstra* was preserved only due to the fact that it was translated into Chinese, as in its motherland, India, no traces of it were found. Japanese scholar Hakuji Ui translated the Chinese text into English in the early 20th century.

Recently, another Japanese scholar, Keiichi Miyamoto, suggested a new translation, as well as a reconstruction of the Sanskrit text. He wrote in the Preface to his book of 2007: "We are now completely free from the worse translation of the text by Dr. Hakuji Ui which has perplexed students of Indian philosophy for eighty years" (3). The authors of this paper intend to translate the *Daśapadārthaśāstra* into Russian, using both Chinese translations as well as the Sanskrit reconstruction of the text, proposed by Miyamoto. At the same time we also propose to conduct a cross-cultural research into the origins of atomism.

The history of the *Daśapadārthaśāstra* is full of mysteries: why has it been erased from the historical memory in India? Why was it selected by the Chinese Buddhist pilgrim from among the other non-Buddhist philosophical texts? These and other important questions of historical and philosophical order we will leave aside in this paper. The place and significance of this text in the history of the Vaiśeṣika school or in the history of Indian philosophy would call for a separate discussion.

How did it happen that this text attracted our attention? Victoria Lysenko, a specialist in Indian philosophy, came across it around twenty years ago while studying the Vaiśeṣika atomism. It turned out that the other author of this paper, Artem Kobzev, a specialist in Chinese philosophy was at that time elaborating his ideas about the specific Chinese mode of philosophical thinking, trying to detect the reasons for an absence in it of some fundamental Western distinctions and oppositions like idealism-materialism, etc. The absence of atomism in traditional Chinese thought had also attracted his attention. The fact that the text of the traditional Brahmanical school containing atomistic formulations was translated into Chinese gave a new turn to his reflections. There was an interesting question to discuss: why did this text not stimulate the interest of Chinese thinkers for atomism? The fact that traditional Chinese thought "did not notice" the atomistic ideas of the Vaiṣeśika text has become an important argument in favor of his hypothesis, that atomism could not be developed in China because of a specifically Chinese style of thinking, determined by the hieroglyphic writing system.

Since that time, each of us has continued to think about the origin and the nature of atomism in its own field of research. With the passing of time, our paths crossed again over this marginal Vaiṣeśika text. However, its importance in our eyes increased immensely as we came along parallel paths to the idea of the linguistic origins of atomism. What do we mean by that? We assume that the idea of extremely small finite and indivisible basic elements making up all things is somehow connected with the fact that it was formulated in the intellectual traditions expressing themselves in the Indo-European languages. Why these two languages but not the others? Because Sanskrit and the Ancient Greek both afford a possibility of reduction of the word lexical level to the level of meaningless sounds and letters, structured on the basis of a purely formal atomistic principle.

As far as our understanding of alphabetical principle is concerned, we have different approaches. Artem Kobzev argues that the birth of the idea of alphabet on the eastern Mediterranean coast at the turn of 2nd and 1st millennium B.C.E. was so relevant to the Indo-European language that this idea was not only practically implemented in all kinds of writing, but also formed the basis of linguistic theories, according to which the ultimate unit of speech was considered as an artificially-singled-out sound, but not as a naturally audible syllable. In his opinion, it is on the basis of the written character that the sound was differentiated.

As for Victoria Lysenko, she understands the alphabetic principle in a more general sense, not attached exclusively to writing. For her, it works as a system of differentiation with regard to speech sounds, as a classification of the ultimate speech units fit for further constructing. Indian oral exegetical tradition of the Vedic ritualistic formulas (*ric, mantras*) gives an example of a differentiation of sounds based exclusively on the modes of their articulation. The production of sound was understood as a contact of the passive places of articulation, or *sthana* (Kaṇṭhya: Velar, Tālavya : Palatal, Mūrdhanya: Retroflex, Dantya: Dental, Ōshtya: Labial and some others) with the active instruments *karaṇa* (*hvāmūla*: tongue root for velar, *Jihvāmadhya*: tongue body, for palatal; *Jihvāgra*: tip of tongue, for cerebral and dental; *Adhōṣṭa*: lower lip, for labial). So, the Indian alphabetic system, according to her, is based on the introspection of tactile feelings in the mouth and on the hearing. The preponderance of hearing over seeing is a crucial factor for the Indian linguistic tradition, based on the highly developed mnemonic techniques.

When we came to grips with this issue, it soon became clear that the idea of atomism as connected with the structure of language had been already launched

50 years ago. It is symptomatic that the person who introduced it, too, sought an inspiration, or rather, a counterexample, in Chinese traditional culture. This was the famous sinologist Joseph Needham. He refers to the parallel between the limitless variety of words that can be built from the relatively few letters of the alphabet, and to the idea that a very small number of elementary particles could, in a multitude of combinations, engender the limitless variety of material bodies (26). Explaining why atomism never really took root in China, Needham observes that the Chinese written character is an organic whole, a Gestalt, and minds accustomed to an ideographic language would perhaps hardly have been so open to the idea of an atomic constitution of matter. As Needham points out, however, the Chinese tradition recognized the function of the atomic principle in numerous contexts, for example the reduction of written characters to radicals, the composition of melodies from the notes of the pentatonic scale, and the representation of Nature through the permutations and combinations of the broken and unbroken lines in the hexagrams of their ancient work of divination the "Yi jing" or "Zhou yi" (26).

An opposing principle of continuity, connected with hieroglyphics in China, was proposed by Artem Kobzev in a 1994 monograph. Another very authoritative, like-minded, scholar-academician, Vyach. Vsevolodovich Ivanov, wrote in his preface to Kobzev's book:

> particularly valuable to me seem the comments on the ideas of Greek science (and throughout the European tradition, to date, which continue what was begun by the Greeks) primarily associated with the concept of letters and the

> alphabet as a system, a part of which a letter constitutes. Naturally, the hieroglyphic nature of ancient Chinese culture has contributed to some of its orientations, in a sense opposite to the alphabetical principle. (6)

Kobzev argues that the Chinese tradition, dominated by a naturalistic and holistic paradigm, did not develop either its own idealism, or its own atomism. It is this omnipotent hieroglyphics that, according to him, became a symbol of all Chinese culture-wen. He explains that hieroglyphs, being full-fledged words, could not be derived from any primary written characters, as far as they are themselves primary elements, in the same vein, as letters. Most of them can be analyzed into component parts, but these parts are themselves hieroglyphs. In addition, the opposition between simplicity of letters and complexity of words does not work here, because some hieroglyphs consisting of one line only are more "simple" than any letter.

Since the end of the 4th century the Buddhist Chinese tradition possessed some information about Indian atomism as fixed in its canonical texts, and by the VIIth century Chinese Buddhists already had a representative picture of its apology and criticism. The *Daśapadārthaśāstra* was included in the Chinese *Tripitaka Da zang jing* (*The Great Treasure of the Canons*).

The Vaiṣeśikas explained the transformation of the atoms into observable objects with the help of numerology, based on combinations of dyads (*dvyaṇuka*) and triads (*tryaṇuka*), numbers 2, 3, and 6. In particular, at the beginning of the *Daśapadārthaśāstra* Hui-yue states that "thin / small body / entity" (wei-ti 微 体) and "short" (duan-ti 短 体) are atomically binary (er-wei-guo 二 微 果), and "large" (da-ti 大体) and "long" (chang-ti 长 体) are atomically ternary (san-wei-ti 三 微 果). Moreover, this theory was presented by Kui-ji 窥基 (632-682) in his comments on the commentary of his teacher Xuan-zang to the famous treatise of Vasubandhu (Shi-qin 世 亲), *Viṃśatika* (*Twenty Verses*): *Wei-shi er-shi lun shu-ji* 唯识 二十 论述 记 (*Notes of Interpretations to Shastra in Twenty* [verses] *of Only Consciousness*). According to Kui-ji, the primary element is the atomic pair ("father" and "mother"), generating a "son" by attaching the atom and becoming a triad. Then two triads are coupled, creating a sixfold combination to which the seventh atom is attached. Next, two sixfold combinations are coupled and to them the fifteenth atom is attached (See Figure 1).

Kobzev brings the comment of Kui-ji into correlation with the binary generative structure that is central to the Chinese methodology (see Figure 2). Its presentation is the description of the 15 phases of the transformation from the Supreme Ultimate (tai-ji 太极) to the eight trigrams (ba-gua 八卦) in the "Yi jing" ("Xi-ci zhuan" - "Tradition of Connected Aphorisms," I, 11) as well as its illustration in the 15 members of the "Image of the linear sequence of eight trigrams according to Fu-xi" ("Fu-xi ba-gua ci-xu tu"; see Figure 3). In both cases, the total number of described structural elements is 15, embodying the most important Chinese numerological structure san-yi ("3 and 5 / triad and pentad / trinity and quinary"):

Figure 1

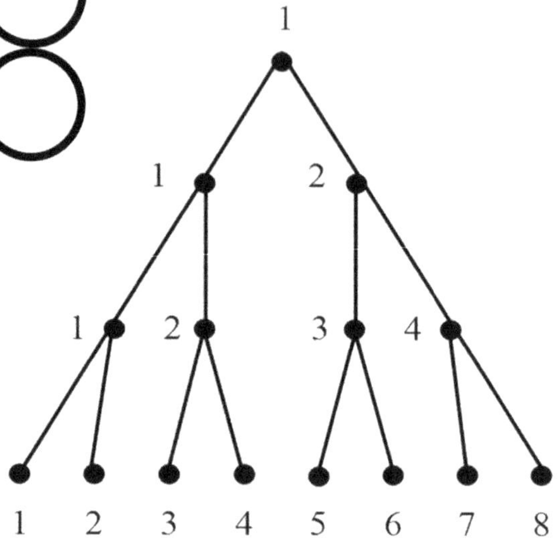

Figure 2

<table>
<tr><td>*Kun*
(15)</td><td>*Gen*
(14)</td><td>*Kan*
(13)</td><td>*Xun*
(12)</td><td>*Zhen*
(11)</td><td>*Li*
(10)</td><td>*Lui*
(9)</td><td>*Qian*
(8)</td></tr>
<tr><td colspan="2">*Tai-yin*
(7)</td><td colspan="2">*Shao-yang*
(6)</td><td colspan="2">*Shao-yin*
(5)</td><td colspan="2">*Tai-yang*
(4)</td></tr>
<tr><td colspan="4">*Yin*
(3)</td><td colspan="4">*Yang*
(2)</td></tr>
<tr><td colspan="8">*Tai-ji*
(1)</td></tr>
</table>

Figure 3

The mechanism for the formation of the bodies from their constitutive atoms is as follows: one atom of the first (top) gives rise to the level of the dyad (two atoms of the second level), which together with it becomes a triad. Two triads (two atoms of the second level and four atoms of the third level) engender a sixfold combination becoming a sevenfold together with an atom of the first level. Two sevenfold combinations (two atoms of the second level, four of the third and eight of the fourth levels) give rise to a combination of fourteen atoms together with the fifteenth atom on the first level. Artem Kobzev suggests that the concept of the Vaiṣeśika may have been under some Chinese influence, particularly its most powerful and original numerologeme – the hexagram (*gua* 卦), is built on the numbers 2, 3 and 6 (2 traits, 2 trigrams, 3 diagrams, 6 positions). He believes that by this way (as he says: through the prophets not accepted in their homeland) the atomistic potential of hexagrams, marked by J. Needham, was realized.

What were the schemes of the atom-based production of bodies in the Vaiṣeśika tradition itself? We have two of them. One is being exposed in the *Daśapadārthaśāstra*, according to which, two atoms generate a dyad, three atoms a triad etc. The other one is presented as a development of Prashastapāda's ideas by his commentator Shridhara (10th century): two atoms constitute a dyad, and three dyads, a triad. It is not clear who introduced this innovation—Prashastapāda, who lived in the 6th century and composed the most authoritative Vaiṣeśika treatise *Padārthadharmasamgraha* ("The Collection of the Characteristics of Categories"), or Shridhara himself?—and whether or not this innovation was connected with the impact from the Chinese interpretation? The study of *Daśapadārthaśāstra* and the developments of Buddhist atomism in China show that Chinese thinkers, even as Buddhists, remained within the traditional numerological framework of hexagrams and assimilated atomism through their prism.

What does the story of *Daśapadārthaśāstra* in China tell us? It clearly indicates that the reception of the ideas of one tradition in another tradition is not possible if in the latter there are no appropriate linguistic conceptual tools. The idea of the atom appears in two very different cultures - the Greek one and the Indian one – as we suppose – largely due to the fact that these cultures express themselves in Indo-European languages. The bearers of these languages were capable of isolating and identifying meaningless but repeatable and unchangeable syllables, including those represented by a single vowel. The words could be forcibly reduced to senseless letters or articulated sound (*varṇas*) in the same way as matter could be reduced to atoms. We cannot confidently assert either that the doctrine of atoms was coined in each of these cultures independently of one another, or that it was invented in one and borrowed by the other. But this does not matter, since in both cases, the common letter-based speech paradigm may play its mediating role. In contrast, the hieroglyphic Chinese culture has traditionally maintained a representation of the linguistic primacy of the syllable as a phonetic equivalent of a hieroglyph. The Chinese could not fix by their characters any meaningless articulated sound.

Some contemporary authors argue that Indian atomism is derived from Greece. Keiichi Miyamoto believes that atomism infiltrated into India through the Bactrian Greeks. This hypothesis gives rise to many questions, such as, why there was no semantic calque of the term "atom," like "indivisible," or "uncut"? The Sanskrit term for atom is *aṇu*, or *paramaṇu*, meaning "small," "tiny," or "thin." But even if we accept the borrowing it does not disprove our linguistic hypothesis. Rather, it confirms it, and in this case, again, we can refer to the total neglect by the traditional non-Buddhist Chinese thought of the Chinese translation of the Vaiṣeśika text. When an idea falls into alien soil, it does not necessarily germinate. Concerning the possibility of a Greek atomistic fertilization of Indian thought, the situation was quite different: the Indian soil was already prepared for it and easily assimilated atomism as an element of its own intellectual culture. Why? According to our suppositions, the Indian soil was ready not only because of the structural similarities of Greek and Sanskrit as languages of one Indo-European group, but also because in India from ancient times there existed a set of linguistic sciences:—grammar (*vyākaraṇa*), phonetics (*çikshā*), and etymology (*nirukta*)—which already developed what may be called "an atomistic approach": the construction of complex linguistic objects from the simplest ones, word-forms from phonemes and morphemes.

But even this was not enough. For the emergence of philosophical atomism, as we believe, some set of more general principles is required: conceptual distinctions, problematizations, and models. In Sanskrit and in Greek we find evidence of similar mental work; in both languages the conceptual distinctions were made between being and becoming, the existence and the process, cause and effect, part and whole, being and nothingness, as well as between the property and its carrier (substance and quality, substance and movement, quality and movement, subject and object, space and time, etc.). These linguistic and conceptual distinctions contributed to the emergence of problems that, in their turn, led to the formulation of the "atomistic hypothesis." It seems that philosophical atomism appears not only as a kind of a new idea, but at the points of discontinuities and inconsistencies of some other explanatory schemes.

In her paper on the linguistic hypothesis of atomism, Victoria Lysenko shows that the key elements of the problem field in which Greek and Indian atomic theories arise and develop are quite similar. What are they? We have not enough time to develop this further on, so we will mention just the most important one: the opposition between the ideas of eternal, unchangeable being and ever-changing becoming (Eleats in Greece, and the teachings designated in the Buddhist texts as *sassatavāda (*eternalism) in India on one side, pitted against Heraclitus in Greece and the Buddhist theories of *dharmas* and *kshaṇikavāda* in India). She notes that the atomistic theory lies in that part of the "problem field", where the spectra of the these oppositions intersect, where being is preserved at the cost of its multiplication and fragmentation into atoms, but the change is also allowed, and even the emergence and destruction are possible, but only in a form of, respectively, conjunction and disjunction of these primary substances; the atoms remain nevertheless eternal and immutable "indivisibles." Outside of this "middle" segment of the field, closer to the pole of absolute mutability, the Indian Buddhist tradition places its *kshaṇikavāda* and the Greek one: Anaxagoras, with his infinite divisible "seeds." Both can be considered as some form of atomism in the sense of explaining the whole in terms of ultimate units, although the notion of "atom" as absolutely indivisible unit is absent in them (see Lysenko's "Between Materialism and Immaterialism: Atomism in India and Greece").

In China, according to Kobzev, this philosophical perspective did not receive such a development, because in the naturalistic world view, which was essentially continuous, rather than discrete, consisting of energies, not of substances, of the activities, not of things, it was the idea of a general variability that predominates, as it was perpetuated in the title of the Chinese book of books – "Yi jing", or "Canon of Changes" (for details, see Kobzev's "China and Correlations between Hieroglyphics and Continualism, Alphabet and Atomism").

Works Cited

Kobzev, Artem I. *Učenie O Simvolach I Čislach V Kitajskoj Klassičeskoj Filosofii (Teaching about Symbols and Numbers in Traditional Chinese Philosophy)*. Moskva: Vostočnaja Literatura, 1994.

———. "Kitay i Vzaimosvyazi Ieroglifiki s continualizmom, a Alfavita s Atomizmom (China and Correlations between Hieroglyphics and Continualism, Alphabet and Atomism)." *XLI Nauchnaya Konferenciya "Obshestvo i Gosudarstvo v Kitaye" (41st Scientific Conference: "Chinese Society and State")*. Moscow: Oriental Literature, 2011. pp. 314-325.

Lysenko, Victoria. "Between Materialism and Immaterialism: Atomism in India and Greece." *Materialism and Immaterialism in India and the West: Varying Vistas*. New Delhi: Project of History of Indian Science, Philosophy and Culture, Centre for Studies in Civilizations, 2010. pp. 253-268.

Miyamoto, Keiichi. *The Metaphysics and Epistemology of the Early Vaiśeşika: With an Appendix Daśapadārthī of Candramati*. Pune, 1996; and *Daśapadārthī: An Ancient Indian Literature of Thoroughly Metaphysical Realism*. Kyoto, 2007.

Needham, Joseph. *Science and Civilization in China. Volume 4: Physics and Physical Technology, Book 1*. Cambridge: Cambridge UP, 1962.

Ui, Hakuju. *Vaiṣeśika Philosophy According to the Daśapadārthaśāstra. Chinese Text with Introduction, Translation and Notes*. London, 1917.

Dr. Artem I. Kobzev is a Professor and Head of Section for Chinese Ideology and Culture at the Institute of Oriental Studies, Russian Academy of Sciences, Moscow.

Dr. Victoria Lysenko is a Professor and head of Department of Oriental Philosophy at the Institute of Philosophy of the Russian Academy of Sciences, Moscow.

CHAPTER 5

VYACHESLAV Y. BELOKRENITSKY

The Western Tribal Region in South Asia: The Limits of Our Knowledge

South Asia is commonly considered a region which includes seven countries: India, Pakistan, Bangladesh, Nepal, Sri Lanka, Bhutan and the Maldives. Despite the fact that Afghanistan became a full member of the South Asian Association for Regional Cooperation (SAARC) in 2006, it is not usually considered a part of the region. Thus, Pakistan is usually treated as the western-most country of the region, and the South Asian tribal area is confined to the territories of this country inhabited by the Pashtun (Pushtun) and Baluchi (Balochi) tribes (see Figure 1).

Strictly speaking, as both the Pashtun and Baluchi belts extend from Pakistan westward to Afghanistan and Iran, the western boundary of South Asia should be drawn somewhere there. But in this logic a doubt arises as to whether this tribal territory belongs to South Asia at all. Topographically, the South Asian western border belt can be easily identified as coinciding with the Indus plains, while the hilly and des-

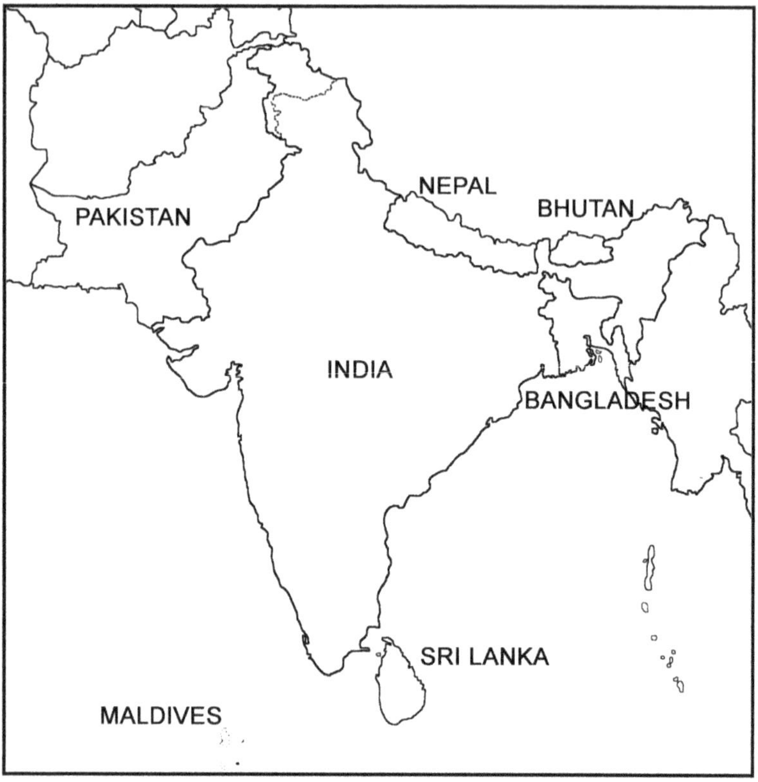

Figure 1: The traditional view of South Asia

ert tracts to the west of the plains belong to another geographical and cultural region which can be named West or South-West or even Mid-West Asia (see Figure 2). And then a broad tribal area of some 800,000 square kilometers emerges as the habitat of the Pashtun and Baluchi tribes, encompassing a large area of Pakistan, plus the southern and eastern provinces of Afghanistan and the Iranian province (*ostan*) of Seistan and Baluchistan (see Figure 3).

This observation notwithstanding, I will concentrate chiefly on Pakistan's tribal areas, touching upon a minimum number of issues pertaining to Afghanistan, particularly its Pashtun region. It should be mentioned

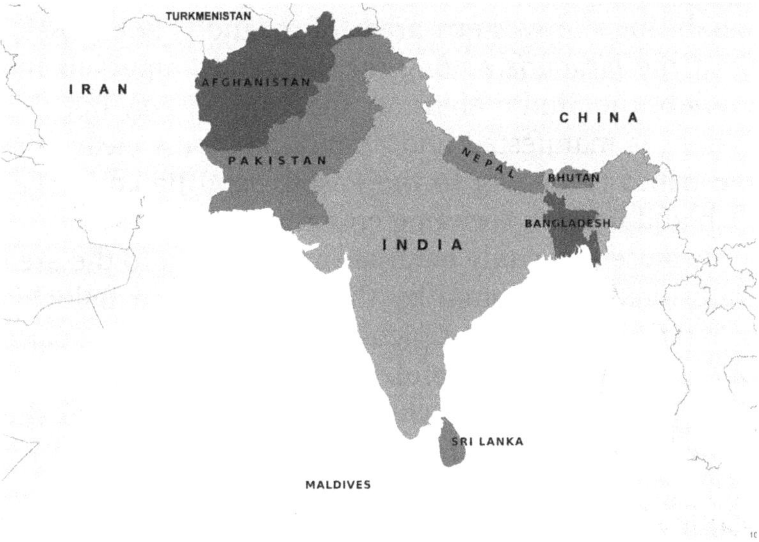

Figure 2: West/South-West/Mid-West Asia

that, historically, the center of the Pashtun tribal area was located in Afghanistan and, geopolitically, both territories have recently become very closely tied. On the ground, however, the Pashtun region often overlaps the contemporary state frontiers. For the Baluchi area, its demographic center lies in Pakistan, and it is discussed here chiefly in respect to the situation in this country. To be precise, the Baluchi area is constituted not only by the Baluchi, but also by the Brahui tribes. From a linguistic point of view, the Brahuis constitute a separate population from the Baluchis; nevertheless, they culturally identify themselves fully with the Baluchis. The Kashmiri north-western part of the region, which has its own composite structure and specific features, is not addressed in this study.

It should be mentioned parenthetically that certain elements of the tribal, agnatic, patrilineal system (married women retain affiliation with their parents' clan) exist among almost all ethnic quasi-primordial groups inhabiting the western areas of extended South Asia, be it the *biradaris* among the Jats and Rajputs of the Punjab, the Sindhi clans, or the Tajik *avlods*. But this system is manifested and maintained most clearly by the tribes belonging to the Pashto- and Baluch- (Baloch and Brahui) speaking communities.

Because this study confines itself chiefly to the area traditionally inhabited by the Pashtuns and Baluchis of Pakistan, a clear-cut picture of the constituent parts of the area may be helpful. Administratively it consists of two provinces: Baluchistan (Balochistan), and the former North-West Frontier Province, which was renamed as Khyber-Pakhtunkhwa (KP) in 2010. Of special interest is the middle belt of the Pashtun territory, called the Federally Administered Tribal Area (FATA). It is comprised of the most hilly and rugged region inhabited by the so-called independent tribes, and divid-

Figure 3: Baluchistan

ed into seven Political Agencies, namely (moving from north to south) Bajaur, Mohmand, Khyber, Orakzai, Kurram, North Waziristan and South Waziristan.

The topicality of the problems presented here seems obvious, as from the scholarly point of view this is one of the few more or less intact tribal zones in Asia. The Pashtun tribal system is probably the largest and most coherent in the world. Pashtun tribes have long attracted intense attention and curiosity, while their origin is now widely discussed and debated in connection with their putative Jewish roots.

From the contemporary practical or political point of view, the region is of profound importance, as it continues to be a safe haven for militants and extremists, and is a major hotbed of internal conflict and international military and peace-keeping operations.

This paper is divided into three parts. The first part briefly presents and discusses the main sources of our knowledge about the tribes and tribal areas. The middle section is dedicated to certain issues surrounding the inadequate knowledge which we have about the tribal areas and the contemporary state of affairs there. The final section further elaborates some problems which present-day scholarship faces concerning our understanding of the social and political realities in the region. This section deals predominantly with the Pakistani areas, and the Pashtun and Baluchi nationalism there.

Knowledge

We presume to know quite a bit about the history of the Pashtuns and Baluchis (the latter to a lesser degree). There is a 200-year tradition of outside observers studying the tribal societies of the region. The process began in the 19th century with the pioneering work by a high-ranking British colonial administrator, Mountstuart Elphinstone. His *An Account of the Kingdom of Caubul* was first published in 1815.[1] This was a treatise prepared after his visit to Afghanistan at the head of the first mission to the court of the Kabul ruler Shah Shuja; it contains a description of the major tribes inhabiting the country, some notes on the history of Afghanistan and the areas (the Tartary) to the north of the boundaries of the Kabul Emirate. The account of the tribes Elphinstone mentions resembles to a considerable extent the concurrent and the present- day nomenclature of major tribes and their places of living.

In the 1820s the third director of the Asian Museum in St. Petersburg, Dr. Bernhard Dorn, translated from the Persian *A History of Afghans*, a work compiled by a chronicler at the court of the Mughal emperor Aurangzeb named Nimatullah Makhzan-i-Afghani. The book contained the putative genealogy of the Afghans (Pashtuns), beginning with the legendary ancestor of all Afghans, Kais bin Rashid, and the lineages of the tribes traced to his four sons. In the end of the 19th and the beginning of the 20th century, several contributions to our knowledge of the Pashtun and Baloch borderlands were made by a number of colonial officers and professionals like H.W. Bellew, T.L. Pennell, and others.[2]

In the second half of the 20th century, after the creation of Pakistan, some social anthropologists and ethnographers started their work in the region. The most significant work was done by Dr. Fredrik (Frederick) Barth, who published his oft-quoted study of the Pashtuns of Swat in 1959, along with several articles on the Pathan-Baluchi boundary in the first half of the 1960s.[3]

A decade later another Pakistani anthropologist, Akbar S. Ahmed, became widely known. He began his research while he was a Political Agent in the Tribal Areas. His most important work, published in 1980, was based on his studies of the Mohmand tribe, which occupied territory on both sides of the Pakistan/Afghanistan frontier (known as the Durand Line). But before these works, he published a number of articles and books on the Pashtuns or Pathans (a synonym widely used in India and elsewhere) of the border region.[4]

Some works of importance were after that written by European specialists like Richard Tapper, Bernt Glatzer and others, though they were to a considerable extent based on secondary material.[5] One of the few exceptions is a field study of Pakistani Pashtuns by an American anthropologist, Charles Lindholm, done in the late 1970s.[6] Generally the conditions were not favorable for conducting field research in the border regions of Pakistan and Afghanistan in the 1990s and 2000s. Some field work was performed after the end of the Taliban rule in 2001, although the bulk of this research was restricted to interviews and observations by scholars or journalists. The preface to the 2007 edition of the *American Tribal Analysis Center* publishing studies done by the Peshawar University Area Study Center illustrates this: "Swat, for example, has become so dangerous that Frederick Barth's studies only could be repeated at the risk of the investigator's life."[7] Similar conditions exist in the Federally Administered Tribal Areas (FATA) and beyond the frontier, in Afghanistan.

Let me mention very briefly what we do know about the Pashtun tribal system. It is acephalous, and democratic in a primitive, primordial sense. All "real" Pashtun adult males treat themselves as equal, and respect traditionally is paid to the elderly wise men, the white-bearded *speen giri*, but these elders are not usually leaders in all matters and for all purposes. Influence and power are shared, and the *Jirga* of the elders (or of all the male members in a smaller tribal community) is the decision maker or arbiter for the tribe. Their decisions are based on the oral traditions, which are codified as the *Pashtunwali* or *Pakhtunwali.*[8] The code is complex and varies, to some extent, from one locality to another but the major principles are: *badal* (revenge, vendetta), *melmastia* (hospitality), and *nanawati* (offering sanctuary to an offender if he accepts his guilt and seeks forgiveness).[9] The overpowering principle is *gairat* (honor), which is associated closely with the dictum of male integrity and independence, and female chastity and modesty.

The most important political institution among the Pashtun tribes is the *Jirga*, an assembly or party which meets for consultation. The *Jirgas* assemble in a *hujra* (village guest house), a village mosque, or in an open field outside the village. The *Jirga* exercise both judicial and executive roles to settle all disputes concerning the distribution of land, properties, blood feuds, etc.[10]

Two types of Pashtun tribes are usually singled out. The *Nang* (meaning "honor") type correspond more to hill tribes observing strictly the ideal Pashtun code of behavior. They primarily inhabit the genuine present-day core of the Pashtun region (i.e., the FATA) and the adjacent Afghan border territories. The *Qalang* ("tax" or "tributory") type is characterized as less strict in adhering to the Pashtun code. The *qalang* tribes are commonly despised by the *nang* tribes, as the *qalang* are dependent on a non-Pashtun social environment, pay taxes to the state, and accept regular subsidies. Thus, they are not independent from an outside authority. The *qalang* tribesmen reside chiefly in the so-called settled districts of the frontier province of Pakistan (Khyber-Pakhtunkhwa) and in similar parts of Afghanistan, which are conducive for combining sheep and goat breeding with agriculture, as it is partly irrigated in the plains and river valleys.

The *qalang* communities may be characterized as being in an initial stage of detribalization. They are the main source for the partly or wholly detribalized Pashtun living in small and larger towns, aspiring for education and work in the outer world. They are the actual and potential emigrants forming part of the temporary labor force working in the non-Pashtun areas of Pakistan and abroad, mainly in the Gulf.

While the mountainous Pashtuns are patriarchal and primordially democratic, building up their organizational structure from below to above, the great masses of Pashtuns residing in the plains and valleys between the mountain ranges have to a greater extent lost their primitively democratic nature. Since the formation of the Afghan tribal empire-state in the middle of the eighteenth century, the Afghans are loosely divided into two big tribal confederacies of a centralized nature, namely the *Durrani* (originally *Abdali*) and the *Ghilzai*.[11]

Associated with the sometimes rather vague remnants of these entities, and partly superseding them, there exist now more than 50 big tribes, each divided into sub-tribes, clans and sub-clans. The total number of these entities in both Pakistan and Afghanistan is estimated to be around 400. The more well-known of the mountainous independent tribes are the Afridi, Mohmand, Mehsood, Wazir, Zadzi, Zadran, Mangal, and Shinwari. The self-identity and integrity of these tribes are based on their perceived genealogy, but as an exception to this rule we have tribes or groups of tribes named after localities like Wardak, Khosti or Khostwal in Afghanistan, and the Marwati and Bunerwal in Pakistan.[12]

The scholarly tradition for the study of the Baluchis is not so deep and extensive. The most important contributions to the field in the contemporary (post-WWII) period were made by American anthropologist Sylvia Matheson as well as by R. N. Perhson and P. Titus.[13]

Unlike the Pashtuns, the Baluchi tribes are cephalous or autocephalous, organized from top to bottom in a hierarchical manner. The highest level of community is a *tuman,* led by a *tumandar* or *Nawab*. *Tumans* are divided into clans (*paras*). Each clan is led by a chief (*mukadam*). *Paras* are further divided into subclans called *palis* or *phallis*, each led by a headman, sometimes named *wadera*. *Palis* may be divided into big family groups led by an elder, who may be known as *motabar*. Tribe, clan or division heads are often referred to as *Sardars*.[14]

Each *tuman* is a separate tribe. The total number of them has been changing with the passage of time and, according to some sources, there are now 24 *tuman.* The most well-known are the Bugti and Marri (Baluchi) tribes. They are the largest tribes, with deep traditions of resistance to outside authority, whether British or Pakistani. On the opposite end of the ideological spectrum are the Raisani, Jamali, and Magsi tribes, with the traditional pro-authority inclination of their elite.

In between the northern (eastern by dialect) Baluchi tribes of the so-called Suleimani group (residing traditionally in the region adjacent to the *Takht-i-Suleiman* or the Suleiman range) and the southern (western by dialect) tribes called Makrani, or coastal, we find Brahui tribes occupying the central parts of the Baluchistan province. Their language is Dravidian, therefore they inherited the language of the Dravids who once inhabited all of India. Physically (anthropologically) they are considered to be of Turko-Iranian extraction. The Brahuis, as mentioned above, identify themselves as Baluchis. The family of the former Khan of Kalat, who supervised other princely states in Baluchistan (Kharan, Makran, and Las-Bela), was Brahui by mother tongue. Many Baluchis and Brahuis are bilingual or trilingual. They often use Seraiki as their household language. The most populous Brahui tribe is Mengal. Its leaders used to play a vanguard role in the Baluchi national movement.

Several Baluchi tribes are found in the southern provinces of Afghanistan (Nimroz, Helmand). They are mostly nomads preserving their traditional way of living. In comparison with the rather miniscule number of Afghani Baluchis, the Iranian Baluchis are greater in number and importance. Some of the Baluchi tribes, like the Naushervani, live on both sides of the Pakistani-Iranian border.

A significant difference between the Pashtun and Baluchi tribal systems lies in the customs of adoption studied by F. Barth and some other anthropologists. This distinction was known to the first generation of researchers. In a 1912 review, A.Baines wrote: "Amongst the Pathans the tribe is more closely knit, and the bond is kinship in the male line. As amongst the Baluch, however, strangers are admitted to qualified membership, tending, in time, to be treated, by fiction, as kinship."[15] The difference can be easily explained by the dissimilarities in the habitat and ways of earning the means for survival. The Pashtuns usually were cautious in taking responsibility for those seeking their constant protection, although with the expansion of their writ and power the number of so-called *hamsaya* (literally, "living under one's shadow") had been increasing. What mattered for the Baluch was their fighting strength. The biggest Baluchi tribe, the Marri, included into their ranks the clan of Bijarani, whose Pashtun origins were well-known. Through this liberal policy of absorbing and adopting, the Marris have grown to be one of the most powerful among the Baluchis.[16]

Inadequate Knowledge

The present-day demographic picture of these tribal areas is one of the major gaps in our knowledge here. This picture is important because projections based upon it impact local, national, and international politics, especially the often-demanded assessment of the strength and perspectives of Pashtun nationalism. This lack of established and widely-accepted figures is addressed by certain estimates and guesses. The most important fact following from the analysis of them is that the majority of the Pashtuns reside now not in Afghanistan, but in Pakistan. This population shift occurred during the 1960s and 1970s, due largely to the effect of the huge man-made irrigation system in the Indus Valley and comparatively better living conditions affecting the death rates in two countries.

The resulting faster growth of the overall population in Pakistan and was reflected in its Pashtun population as well. According to the latest estimates, about 180 million people reside permanently in Pakistan and 30 million in Afghanistan. The Pashtun population constitutes around 15% of the Pakistani population, or 27 to 28 million people. There are different assessments of the percentage which constitute the Pashtuns in Afghanistan. The most accepted guess for the Pashtun population of Afghanistan is 40 to 42 %, which gives us a figure of between 12 and 13 million people. The overall number of Pashtuns, then, is about 40 million, with twice as many living in Pakistan as in Afghanistan.[17]

The majority of the Pashtun population in Afghanistan is settled in the south (the Durrani tribes) and the east (the Ghilzai tribes). Some Pashtuns traditionally reside in the south-west, near Herat (the Durrani clan of the Nurzai, among others) and some in the northern part, mainly in the province of Kunduz.

In Pakistan around 4 million Pashtun inhabit the FATA (which is 2.5 % of the population, based on the data of the latest census, which was conducted in 1998), and about 18 million reside in the former North-West Frontier (now Khyber-Pakhtunkhva province). According to the 1998 census, 13% of the total Pakistani population lives in this province, of which 75% are Pashtuns. Approximately 5 million Pashtun inhabit the northern region of Baluchistan province, and 3 to 4 million are found in some major cities, especially in Karachi, the biggest city in the country. Karachi can be considered today to be the largest Pashtun city in the world.[18]

The number of Baluchis together with Brahuis in Pakistan exceeds 10 million. Out of this population about 7 million reside in the province of Baluchistan, while the rest can be found in the southern districts of Punjab and in the rural and urban Sind. The largest and oldest Baluchi settlement in Karachi is Lyari, along the banks of the river close to the central quarters of the city.[19] A considerable number of Baluchis, some 2 to 3 million, reside in Iran, and less than a million, presumably, in Afghanistan.

According to L. Rzehak, the distinction between Pashtun and Baluch in Afghanistan is sometimes very subtle. Some groups are referred to as Afghan-(Pashtun)-Baluch. These are splinter groups of Pashtun origin which were incorporated into Baluchi tribal organizations or, alternatively, groups of Baluch origin adopted by Pashtuns.[20]

Apart from demography and the precise location of the tribes, we are also lacking in knowledge of contemporary living conditions in the tribal region of South Asia. We can only guess about the conditions on the ground, as they seem to be thoroughly disturbed by the events of more than 30 years of uninterrupted internecine war complicated by the presence of foreign troops. The production of poppy has become a considerable, and in many cases decisive, source of income for the peasantry of the Pashtun south of Afghanistan, primarily the provinces of Helmand and Kandahar. Another factor of significance for the region, especially the FATA and the neighboring territories of Pakistan is migration to the Middle East in search of temporary work. Both of these issues merit further attention from scholars.

Beginning in 2001, the restoration of the norms of life prevailing in Afghanistan before the April (*Saur*) 1978 revolution—which had led to abrupt and rude social upheaval and years of hardship and internal displacements—was both slow and uneven in different regions of this vast and topographically highly fragmented country. The process of returning home from exile is far from complete; an estimated 1.5 million of Afghans (predominantly Pashtuns) are still in Pakistan, with the majority of them living in the FATA.[21]

Within the first decade of this century, life in major

cities and commercial towns under the official Kabul authorities and their outside (U.S. and NATO) protectors restored rather quickly, and acquired definite new modern features. However, rural living conditions continue to be largely determined by archaic forms of production and administered by traditional local forces and old domineering groups of interest overlaid and challenged by growing networks of radically pro-Islamic, fundamentalist Taliban and like-minded forces, which rely upon income from drug production, various other illicit activities, and a steady stream money from external donors and supporters.

The military impasse for the allied forces in Afghanistan made them think of prospects of a retreat.[22] Since 2009, when the U.S. administration announced plans to withdraw the bulk of its combat troops from Afghanistan, the Taliban, headed by Mullah Omar, the former head (*Amir-ul-Momineen*) of the Islamic Emirates of Afghanistan (1996-2001), seemed to bide time in the expectation of this withdrawal of foreign forces. By 2012, they seemingly agreed to talks with the U.S. representatives, which can be seen as an ambiguous portent for the future of the country, as these talks might lead to gradual reconciliation and consolidation of the nation or to a new stage of fratricidal war.

One of the most important unanswered questions in connection with local communities is the extent to which the tribal system still holds. It can be ascertained from some recent publications that, although the tribal organizational and value systems retain their significance, many things have changed. Foremost is the diminished power and influence of the elders, of *maliks* and *knans* (both those elected and those "officially" selected by the state authorities) in many parts of the tribal region. This is especially true of the Pashtun areas in southern and eastern Afghanistan and in the adjacent parts of Pakistan, the FATA, in particular.

Previous studies of the position of these elders have offered the analysis that the power of the elders was based on three interrelated tribal practices:

- The traditional practice of land ownership, and thus, their leading position in the economic sphere coupled with material advantages of relations with the outer "big state" authorities;
- The place they occupied in the councils (*jirgas*) which had the tools to administer internal judicial affairs and to settle problems with neighbors; and
- Their commanding positions in the tribal *lashkars* (militia, or fighting brigades).

In recent decades certain parts of the tribal region most probably underwent profound changes in all three of these aspects. The importance of traditional land ownership has decreased, because it was undermined by the waves of migration and internal displacements. Simultaneously, market relations have been on the rise within these areas, and arable land has been acquiring a growing market value. Thus it can often be sold outside the kinship group. A more or less lucrative poppy cultivation can be one strong factor behind the actual liquidation of the traditional system of collective ownership of land, with remnants of the centuries-old custom of regular exchanges of land plots between different branches and families of the same kinship group (*wesh*) falling prey to the economics of drug cultivation.

Also, the tribal areas seemed to experience the fragmentation of control between the state (Pakistani and Afghan) and the local forces struggling against it. In the ensuing fight, the power of tribal elders was not only challenged by younger leaders–military commanders linked with pro-Islamic radical groups–but they and their families were the first to suffer the loss of life and property.[23] A number of difficult, bloody, and costly skirmishes occurred between the militants (Taliban) and tribal *lashkars*, leaving the *Jirgas* and *lashkars* with varying levels of importance and status among the tribes. Their significance seems to be most elevated in places where relations between neighboring tribes are further complicated by sectarian tensions, as in the Kurram agency of FATA, where the whole of the Turi tribe and a significant number of the Orakzai tribe are Shi'ite.

The influx of new money into the region, both from jihadi sources and the drug trade,[24] along with the continued emigration of young tribesmen to the rich Middle Eastern countries (which began in the 1970s), have both had an adverse influence on the preservation of traditions within the region. While certain traditions have continued with few changes, the tribal Pashtun (and to a lesser degree, Baluch) society, has in some respects changed quite radically. In short, the tribal system plays an important role in isolated and remote places, but has given way during the last three decades to a new shape and structure in the more economically and culturally advanced zones.

Demanded Knowledge

The above-mentioned relationship between traditional and non-traditional power brokers is but a part of the information most urgently needed today, both politically and geopolitically. The problem can be formulated as defining the relations between the tribal system and "warlordism," with both addressing Islamic radicalism.

Agents within the region have ascertained that tribal elders are not the group from which warlords (military commanders) are recruited. The same is true of the rank-and-file militants. The militants, including primarily the Taliban, belong as a rule to the so-called *kashars* (the young, the poor, and those belonging to minor lineages). The social and generational gaps between the tribal elders and the young and dispossessed of the region partly explain the extent of militancy and warlordism in the tribal areas, as well as the mass support of such constructs by younger people aspiring to play a greater role in social, economic, and political life. The elders, on the contrary, attempt to preserve the status quo, especially if they are linked to the mafia of poppy transporters and traffickers.[25]

This does not exclude the phenomenon of the support provided by certain tribes and tribal groups to the militants. For example, Jalaluddin Haqqani's network has a support base among his native Zadran tribe and some other tribes residing in the so-called *Loya Paktiya* (big Paktiya), which is made up of the Afghan provinces of Paktiya, Paktika, and Khost and the North Waziristan agency of the FATA.[26] The Tehrik-e Taliban Pakistan (TTP), which is a rather loose network of Pashtun radicals formed in December 2007, has roots primarily with the tribesmen and kinsmen of their regions. In the FATA agencies of North and South Waziristan they belong mainly to the Mehsuds and Wazirs, especially the Ahmadzai Wazirs. The same is true of separate chapters of the TTP in the central and northern parts of the FATA and of Swat and Buner districts in KP province. Militancy does not coincide strictly with tribal allegiances but relies upon personal ties, although it is rooted, more often than not, in the common tribal background. Islamic extremists and the militants of TTP and other groups are pulling young people who are not only ambitious but also commonly unemployed. Desperate economic conditions also explain to a great extent the spread of militancy and religious fever in the region.

For example, the Mohmand chapter of the TTP has gained significant power due to the disappointment felt by ordinary tribesmen and some tribal chiefs in the efforts of the Pakistani state to improve their lives. This has contributed to the growth of support for militant (Salafi) groups in the Agency. It is remarkable, however, that the majority of the Mohmand tribesmen, who are utterly uneducated and deprived of access to such facilities as clean drinking water, seem to retain the belief that the Pakistan federal government is the only force capable of alleviating their poverty.[27]

Related to this is the question of the link between the Pashtun extremism and professional clerics. To what extent can we attribute the radicalism of the Pashtuns to the role of Islamic professionals and practitioners? Traditionally there were four religious layers in Pashtun society:

a. Saints, or mystics of Sufi orders (*pirs, akhunds*) and shrine keepers;
b. the Sayyeds, claiming to be descendants of the Arabs, relatives and first followers of the Prophet;
c. educated religious teachers (*maulavis*) at madrassas and seminaries; and
d. mullahs or priests in mosques, including small village mosques.

Religious judges—the *kazis* or *kadies*—can also be added to this list, but in many cases the presence of clerics in a region was negligible. Among them, ideological extremism or fundamentalism (salafism) could most easily be found among the teachers in religious schools and clerics in general, as many of them had received training either abroad or in such well-known centers of the Deobandi Sunni sect as Dar-ul-Uloom Haqqaniya in Akora Khattak.

It should also be mentioned that village mullahs were often treated in their communities as on a par with servants (*kamin*). Higher social status was enjoyed by the Sayyeds and the Saints, the holy men of spirit and spiritual knowledge who several times in history spearheaded social and political protest movements.

Present-day extremism is only partly linked to individuals with a religious background. In Islam, everyone can become a preacher and enjoy religious authority, and thus gain followers. So radical Islamists may emerge from a non-religious background, and in reality they did emerge, thanks to the policy begun in the 1980s of sending young tribals to Saudi Arabia and Persian Gulf countries for religious education. Upon their return, many of them opened madrassas in which young tribesmen were indoctrinated to participate in jihad. The spread of Jihadist Salafi ideology was a direct result of such practices.[28]

One more question of great practical importance is the current state and the future prospects of Pashtun nationalism as an ideology and a movement. It's worth recollecting that the banner of a Free or Independent Pashtunistan was raised twice in the 1940s. At first it was used in the period before the referendum in the North-West Frontier Province of British India in July 1947, which was to decide the fate of the province, whether it joined India or Pakistan. Secular Pashtun nationalists, affiliated with the Indian National Congress, put forward the demand to include a third option in the referendum: the creation of an independent

Pashtunistan. The proposal was rejected by the British authorities, and the idea of sovereignty for the NWFP was marginalized after the creation of Pakistan. There was, however, one exception. The Fakir of Ipi, popular among the tribes of Waziristan and known as the leader of the anti-British movement in the 1930s, picked up the banner and in January 1950 proclaimed himself "President of Pashtunistan." His initiative had the backing of the Afghan royal court in Kabul and the support of jailed Ghaffar Khan. The separatist movement in the Pashtun tribal belt was suppressed by attacks of the Pakistan air force, and died out soon with the normalization of Pakistan-Afghan relations and incorporation of Pashtun leaders, including Abdul Ghaffar's brother Khan Sahib, in the political elite of Pakistan.[29]

Since then, the Pashtunistan movement, represented by the party headed by Abdul Ghaffar's son and grandson, has become one political manifestation of the desire for greater provincial autonomy. In the 1970s the movement formed an alliance with the pro-Islam parties popular largely in the remoter parts of the province, but it was more often opposed to them. In 2002, the Islamist bloc of parties (*Muttahida Majlis-e Amal*, the United Front of Action) won the provincial elections and remained in power in the province until the elections of 2008, when the Awami National Party, led by Ghaffar's grandson Asfandyar Khan, won the majority and formed the government.

In the rivalry between secular and religious Pashtun nationalisms, the tribal regions tilted to the latter. This shift became quite evident after the rise of the Taliban in Afghanistan and the subsequent creation of the Pakistani Taliban. As mentioned in the Center for Strategic and International Studies' 2009 report on the situation in FATA, the Taliban have instrumentalized cultural symbols to mobilize the tribals. Pashtun nationalism has been replaced by Islamic nationalism. The Taliban have been fighting for a truly Islamic Pakistan, against the rulers of the country, who have, according to the Taliban, made "Pakistani soldiers American proxies."[30]

Separatist trends within this process have been effectively curbed, subsumed into the image of an ideal Pakistani Islamo-nationalism. This image, then, is used as a platform for expansion based upon the unity of the Pakistani and Afghan Taliban. This unity is especially significant when it is considered against the prevalence of mild forms of regionalism among Pashtuns of the Pakistani plains and cities. Ethno-nationalism, which combines Pashtun solidarity and Islamist ideology, is of course the most dangerous internal threat against the stability of Punjabi-dominated Pakistan. But the current menace seems mitigated by the activities of the Punjabi elite, who (since the 1980s or, perhaps, much earlier) successfully integrated into its ranks the Pashtun elite. The backbone of the present Pakistani integrity is the collusion between or union of the Punjabi and Pashtun elites.

A different story emerges with the Baluch nationalism movement. The Khan of Kalat's refusal to join the new state of Pakistan in 1947 signaled the creation of this essentially separatist movement. The revolt of the Khan's brother in 1948 was crushed by the Pakistani forces which occupied the princely state. The army was brought into Baluchistan again in 1973 and remained there fighting the armed rebellion of the tribes, mainly the Marri, until 1977. In 2003 the army again invaded the province to put down a new rebellion, this time instigated by the Bugti tribe. It remained there even after the tribal chief Nawab Akbar Khan Bugti died in the midst of an army attack in August 2006. The insurgency after that went underground, being politically represented by a string of anti-Pakistan separatist parties headed by representatives of the tribal elite and the urban middle class.[31]

The influence of secular and leftist ideology in Baluchistan was quite strong in the 1970s, and still continues today, although it is now more marginalized. It is largely a thing of the past, but it is not totally forgotten or left behind. The ideology of a left-wing nationalist movement has given way to a more Islamized nationalism. The transformation was not only the fallout from recent geopolitical events in Afghanistan (the Afghan Taliban headquarters are widely considered to be in or near the provincial capital of Quetta), but also due to the growing importance of the sectarian Sunni/Shia rivalry and disturbances caused by it. The Baluchi Sunni militant group Jundallah ("The soldiers of Allah") has surfaced, and has claimed responsibility for the subversive acts committed in Iran. Although known mainly for this campaign, it is also rumored to have links with the Taliban and Al-Qaeda, thus adding Islamist overtones to the previously non-religious, partly separatist and partly autonomist activities.

Simple economics also played into this reality. The province has had a slow rate of economic growth–it possesses the lowest level of socio-economic advancement of any province in Pakistan–and this may explain why the tribal system among the Baluchis has remained to a greater extent unchanged.

Conclusion

The Western region of South Asia is presently the most volatile and unstable part of the former Indian subcontinent. This, to some degree, can be explained by the tribal structure of the society there. In spite of the centuries-long tradition of studying the Pashtun and Baluchi tribes, much remains to be explored and analyzed, for the geopolitical situation in this area is fluid, while at the same time many features of tribal society remain intact.

The most recent history of both Pakistan and Afghanistan is connected with the Islamic movement of Taliban. The short period of their rule in Afghanistan ended in 2001, when the coalition forces of the U.S. and the U.K. invaded the country by air and, with the help of the local Northern Alliance, forced the Taliban from Afghanistan to Pakistan. Certain parts of the latter country became the safe haven for the Talibs, who were defeated but neither disorganized nor physically or morally disarmed.

The revival of the movement started in 2003 after the U.S. invaded the Saddam Husein's Iraq. From 2005 to 2007 the Taliban returned to the southern parts of Afghanistan, and their allies had reestablished their presence in the eastern provinces bordering the mountainous regions of Pakistan. In December 2009, finding no way to defeat the Taliban once again, U.S. President Barack Obama announced the decision to pull out the American troops from Afghanistan, leaving behind only military instructors and training teams to continue to build the Afghanistan national army and the Afghan police. In addition to the instructors and trainees, some forces would also be stationed in Afghanistan to protect the key elements of modern civil and military infrastructure (airbases, bridges, arsenals, etc.) This decision was fully supported by American allies in NATO, some of whom were even more eager to withdraw as soon as possible. The disengagement and pullout of troops began in 2011 and will be completed by the end of 2014.

One of the crucial questions to be raised in the new geopolitical situation is the reaction to these moves of the Taliban and the larger Pashtun society in both Afghanistan and Pakistan. The problems which the Western tribal region of South Asia present seem to be more acute than ever before. What will be the reaction of the Pashtuns residing in the mountainous regions along the frontier between Afghanistan and Pakistan? How is this reaction related to the strength and popularity of the radical Islamic organizations known under the name of Taliban? To what extent will the time-honored old tribal system continue to function, and what will be the role of tribal elders in future? Which changes have actually taken root in the contemporary life of the tribal belt, and what things have remained unchanged, proving to be "change resistant"? These issues can only be addressed through a commitment to new field research, interviews with the people who are familiar with the situation in the secluded tribal territories, by comparison and analysis of the various data and, finally, by monitoring and analyzing attitudes and actions of the people inhabiting the tribal areas.

Notes

1. The full name of the second edition of the book is: *An Account of the Kingdom of Caubol and Its Dependencies in Persia, Tartary, and India, Comprising a View of the Afghaun Nation, and a History of the Douranee Monarchy.* London, 1819 (the first edition appeared in 1815).

2. About the book by Bernhard Dorn, see: Glatzer B. "The Pashtun Tribal System." in *The Concept of Tribal Society*. New Delhi: Concept Publishers, 2002. pp.268-269; Bellew, H.W. *The Races of Afghanistan, Being a Brief Account of the Principal Nations Inhabiting that Country.*

Calcutta: n.p., 1880; and Pennell, T.L. *Among the Wild Tribes of the Afghan Frontier*. Karachi: n.p., 1975. (Reprint of the original London edition, 1909).

3. Barth, Fredrik. *Political Leadership Among Swat Pathans*. London: University of London, Athlone Press, 1959; and Barth, Fredrik. "Ethnic Processes on the Pathan-Baluch Boundary." in Ed. Morgenstierne, Georg. *Indo-Iranica: Melanges Presentes a Georg Morgenstierne a L'occasion de son soixante-dixieme anniversaire*. Wiesbaden: Otto Harrassowitz, 1964; and Barth, Fredrik. "The System of Social Stratification in Swat, North Pakistan." in *Aspects of Caste in South India, Ceylon and North-West Pakistan*. Ed. Leach, Edmund R. Cambridge, Cambridge UP, 1960. pp. 113-146.

4. See Ahmed, Akbar S. *Millennium and Charisma Among Pathans: A Critical Essay in Social Anthropology*. London: Routledge & Kegan Paul, 1976; and Ahmed, *Akbar S. Pukhtun Economy and Society: Traditional Structure and Economic Development in a Tribal Society*. London: Routledge & Kegan Paul, 1980.

5. See "Introduction," by Richard Tapper, in Tapper, Richard, ed. *The Conflict of Tribe and State in Iran and Afghanistan*. London: Croom Helm, 1983. pp. 1-82; Bernt Glatzer. "Is Afghanistan on the Brink of Ethnic and Tribal Disintegration?" in *Fundamentalism Reborn? Afghanistan and the Taliban*. Ed. William Maley. NY: NYU Press, 1998. pp. 167-181; Oberson, José. *Khans and Warlords: Political Alignment, Leadership and the State in Pashtun Society: Anthropological Aspects and the Warlordism Debate*. Bern: s.n, 2002. etc.

6 Lindholm, Charles. *Generosity and Jealousy: The Swat Pukhtun of Northern Pakistan*. New York: Columbia University Press, 1982.

7. See the "Preface" to Taizi, Sherzaman. *Jirga System in Tribal Life*. Peshawar: U of Peshawar Area Study Centre, 2007. p. 1. This publication can be accessed online

at <www.tribalanalysiscenter.com>.

8. Taizi, p. 3-5.

9. See the above mentioned sources and also the most recent comprehensive review paper: Rzehak, Lutz. *Doing Pashto: Pashtunwali As the Ideal of Honourable Behaviour and Tribal Life Among the Pashtuns*. Afghanistan Analysts Network, 2011. <afghanistan-analysts.net/>.

10. Taizi, p. 2.

11. The emerging of the state system based on the Afghan tribal big social entities serving as a blueprint for the statist military-political groupings has been studied by a number of scholars of various schools in the twentieth century. A distinguished place among them is occupied by the Soviet Marxist School, represented by scholars like I.M. Reysner, Y.V.Gankovsky, L.R.Gordon-Polonskaya, V.A.Romodin etc. See, in particular, Gankovsky's almost forgotten masterpiece *Imperiya Durrani* (*The Durrani Empire*) published in 1958.(Moscow: Nauka).

12. For the mythological genealogy of the Pashtun tribes, complex links between them and historically recorded migrations, see the classic work by Olaf Caroe, the last British Governor of the Indian NWFP: Caroe, Olaf. *The Pathans: 550 B.C. - A.D. 1957*. Karachi, 1975 (originally published in London, 1958). On the contemporary composition and habitat of different Pashtun tribes one may refer to some of the aforementioned works as well as several sources in Russian: Basov, V.V. "Plemennoi faktor v politicheskih protsessah sovremennogo Afganistana" ("The Tribal Factor in the Political Processes of Contemporary Afghanistan") in *Afghanistan: problemy voiny i mira* (*Afghanistan: Problems of War and Peace*). Moskva, 2000. pp. 91-93, 102-103. Also: Satsaev E.B. "Pushtuny Afganistana i Pakistana. Rukopis deponirovana v INION." ("The Pashtuns of Afghanistan and Pakistan. A Manuscript Deposited in the Institute

for Social Sciences (INION).” Moscow, 1988.

13. Matheson, Sylvia A. *The Tigers of Baluchistan.* London: Barker, 1967; Pehrson, Robert N, and Fredrik Barth. *The Social Organization of the Marri Baluch.* Chicago: Aldine Pub. Co, 1966; Titus, Paul, ed. *Marginality and Modernity: Ethnicity and Change in Post-Colonial Balochistan.* Karachi: Oxford UP, 1996.

14. *The Baluch and the Brahui and Their Rebellions.* Tribal Analysis Center. Williamsburg, VA: Tribal Analysis Center, 2009. p. 10. This publication can be accessed online at <http://www.tribalanalysiscenter.com>.

15. “Ethnography (Castes and Tribes),” by Sir Athelstane Baines. *Encyclopedia of Indo-Aryan Research.* Strasburg: Karl J. Trubner, 1912. p. 9.

16. Barth, Fredrik. “Ethnic Processes on the Pathan-Baluch Boundary.” rpt. in *The Newsletter of Baluchistan Studies* 7 (Fall 1990): 75.

17. The author can refer to his article published in Russian at the website www.afghanistan.ru (see the label Obshchestvo (The Society) entitled “Grani pushtunskoy tsivilizatsii” (“Characteristics of the Pushtun civilization”) based on an earlier, larger version, “Pushtuny Afganistana i Pakistana” (“The Pashtuns of Afghanistan and Pakistan”) published in the book *Afganistan na perehodnom etape* (*Afghanistan at the Stage of Transition*). Moscow: Institute of Oriental Studies, 2002. pp. 39-68.

18. Based on the census data quoted in: Lieven, Anatol. *Pakistan: A Hard Country.* New York: Public Affairs, 2011. pp. 518-519.

19. For the up-to-date story of the growing population of Karachi see: Hasan, A. *The Unplanned Revolution: Observations on the Processes of Socio-Economic Change in Pakistan.* Karachi: Oxford UP, 2009.

20. Rzehak, Lutz. *Doing Pashto: Pashtunwali As the Ideal of Honourable Behaviour and Tribal Life Among the Pashtuns.* Afghanistan Analysts Network, 2011, p. 6.

The author, who graduated from Leningrad (now St. Petersburg) University in 1985, works in Germany and combines access to literature in Russian, German and English as well as in Dari and Pashto with linguistic and anthropologic fieldwork in Afghanistan in 1988 and between 2002 and 2010. The fieldwork by L. Rzehak can be considered as exceptional and made possible in the periods when the official authorities, backed by the presence of the foreign troops, were in control of the urban centers in the tribal areas.

21. Nawaz, Shuja. *Fata—A Most Dangerous Place: Meeting the Challenge of Militancy and Terror in the Federally Administered Tribal Areas of Pakistan.* Washington, D.C: CSIS Press, 2009. p.1.

22. Dorronsoro, Gilles. *Afghanistan: Searching For Political Agreement.* Washington, D.C.: Carnegie Endowment, 2010. pp. 9-19. <carnegieendowment.org/files/searching_polit_agreement.pdf>.

23. More than 600 tribal maliks in FATA have been assassinated by militants, according to Nawaz, p. 6.

24. Lieven, p. 429.

25. Nawaz, p.22.

26. Gopal, Anand, Mansur Khan Mahsud, and Brian Fishman. "The Battle for Pakistan: Militancy and Conflict in North Waziristan." New America Foundation, 2010. pp. 4-6. <counterterrorism.newamerica.net/publications/policy/the_battle_for_pakistan_north_waziristan>.

27. Khan Raza. "The Battle for Pakistan: Militancy and Conflict in Mohmand." New America Foundation, 2010. p. 1. <counterterrorism.newamerica.net/publications/policy/the_battle_for_pakistan_mohmand>.

28. Mahsud, Mansur Khan. "The Battle for Pakistan: Militancy and Conflict in South Waziristan." New America Foundation, 2010. pp. 1,3. <counterterrorism.newamerica.net/publications/policy/the_battle_for_paki-

stan_south_waziristan>.

29. Belokrenitsky, Vyacheslav Y, and V N. Moskalenko. *A Political History of Pakistan, 1947-2007*. Karachi: Oxford UP, 2012.

30. Nawas, p. 28.

31. Harrison Selig S. "Pakistan's Baluch Insurgency." *Le Monde Diplomatique*, October 2006. <mondediplo.com/2006/10/05baluchistan>.

Works Cited

Ahmed, Akbar S. *Millennium and Charisma Among Pathans: A Critical Essay in Social Anthropology*. London: Routledge & Kegan Paul, 1976.

———. *Pukhtun Economy and Society: Traditional Structure and Economic Development in a Tribal Society*. London: Routledge & Kegan Paul, 1980.

Barth, Fredrik. "The System of Social Stratification in Swat, North Pakistan." *Aspects of Caste in South India, Ceylon and North-West Pakistan*. Ed. Edmund R. Leach. Cambridge: Cambridge UP, 1960. pp. 113-146.

———. "Ethnic Processes on the Pathan-Baluch Boundary." rpt. in *The Newsletter of Baluchistan Studies* 7 (Fall 1990): 75.

———. "Ethnic Processes on the Pathan-Baluch Boundary." *Indo-Iranica: Melanges Presentes a Georg Morgenstierne a L'occasion de son soixante-dixieme anniversaire*. Ed. Georg Morgenstierne. Wiesbaden: Otto Harrassowitz, 1964.

The Baluch and the Brahui and Their Rebellions. Tribal Analysis Center. Williamsburg, VA: Tribal Analysis Center, 2009. p. 10. <www.tribalanalysiscenter.com.>

Behera, Deepak K, and Georg Pfeffer, eds. *The Concept of Tribal Society*. New Delhi: Concept Pub. Co, 2002.

Belokrenitsky, Vyacheslav Y, and V N. Moskalenko. *A Political History of Pakistan, 1947-2007*. Karachi: Oxford UP, 2012.

Caroe, Olaf K. The Pathans: 550 B.C. - A.D. 1957. Karachi: Oxford UP, 1958.

Dorronsoro, Gilles. *Afghanistan: Searching For Political Agreement*. Washington, D.C.: Carnegie Endowment, 2010.

Elphinstone, Mountstuart, Andrew Strahan, John Macartney, and M Thomson. *An Account of the Kingdom of Caubul, and Its Dependencies in Persia, Tartary, and India: Comprising a View of the Afghaun Nation, and a History of the Dooraunee Monarchy*. London: Longman, Hurst, Rees, Orme, and Brown, Paternoster-Row, and J. Murray, Albemarle-Street, 1815.

Glatzer, Bernt. "Is Afghanistan on the Brink of Ethnic and Tribal Disintegration?" *Fundamentalism Reborn? Afghanistan and the Taliban*. Ed. William Maley. NY: NYU Press, 1998. pp. 167-181.

———. "The Pashtun Tribal System." *Concepts of Tribal Society*. Eds. Georg Pfeffer and Deepak Kumar Behera. Delhi: Concept Publishing Co., 2002.

Gopal, Anand, Mansur Khan Mahsud, and Brian Fishman. "The Battle for Pakistan: Militancy and Conflict in North Waziristan." New America Foundation, 2010. <counterterrorism.newamerica.net/publications/policy/the_battle_for_pakistan_north_waziristan>.

Harrison Selig S. "Pakistan's Baluch Insurgency." *Le Monde Diplomatique*. October 2006. <mondediplo.com/2006/10/05baluchistan>.

Hasan, A. *The Unplanned Revolution: Observations on the Processes of Socio-Economic Change in Pakistan*. Karachi: Oxford UP, 2009.

Khan Raza. "The Battle for Pakistan: Militancy and Conflict in Mohmand." New America Foundation, 2010.

<counterterrorism.newamerica.net/publications/policy/the_battle_for_pakistan_mohmand>.

Leach, Edmund R. *Aspects of Caste in South India, Ceylon, and North-West Pakistan.* Cambridge: Cambridge UP, 1960.

Lieven, Anatol. *Pakistan: A Hard Country.* New York: Public Affairs, 2011.

Lindholm, Charles. *Generosity and Jealousy: The Swat Pukhtun of Northern Pakistan.* New York: Columbia UP, 1982.

Mahsud, Mansur Khan. "The Battle for Pakistan: Militancy and Conflict in South Waziristan." New America Foundation, 2010. <counterterrorism.newamerica.net/publications/policy/the_battle_for_pakistan_south_waziristan>.

Matheson, Sylvia A. *The Tigers of Baluchistan.* London: Barker, 1967.

Nawaz, Shuja. *Fata—A Most Dangerous Place: Meeting the Challenge of Militancy and Terror in the Federally Administered Tribal Areas of Pakistan.* Washington, D.C: CSIS Press, 2009. p.1. <csis.org/files/media/csis/pubs/081218_nawaz_fata_web.pdf>.

Oberson, José. *Khans and Warlords: Political Alignment, Leadership and the State in Pashtun Society: Anthropological Aspects and the Warlordism Debate.* Bern: s.n, 2002.

Pehrson, Robert N, and Fredrik Barth. *The Social Organization of the Marri Baluch.* Chicago: Aldine Pub. Co, 1966.

Pennell, T L. *Among the Wild Tribes of the Afghan Frontier: A Record of Sixteen Years Close Intercourse with the Native of the Indian Marches.* Karachi: Oxford University Press, 1975.

Rzehak, Lutz. *Doing Pashto: Pashtunwali As the Ideal of Honourable Behaviour and Tribal Life Among the Pashtuns.* Afghanistan Analysts Network, 2011. <afghani-

stan-analysts.net/>.

Tapper, Richard, ed. *The Conflict of Tribe and State in Iran and Afghanistan*. London: Croom Helm, 1983.

Titus, Paul, ed. *Marginality and Modernity: Ethnicity and Change in Post-Colonial Balochistan*. Karachi: Oxford UP, 1996.

Dr. Vyacheslav Y. Belokrenitsky is a Professor and Deputy Director of the Institute of Oriental Studies of the Russian Academy of Sciences, Moscow.

CHAPTER 6

JAMAL MALIK

Modernity, Diversity, and the Public Sphere: Negotiating Religious Identities in 18th-20th Century India. Some Ideas on Pre-Colonial Modernity: The Case of the Indian Muslim Pietists[1]

In the following I will revisit discourses of Muslim scholars and mystics in 18th-century urban North India in order to discuss the possibility for new research in religious individualization, entangled histories, and indigenous modernity. Examples of shared histories are the simultaneous occurrence of messianism around the Mediterranean and in South Asia in the 16th century, and the international use of "fundamentalisms" in the last quarter of the 20th century. Such a situation can also be seen in the 18th century, a period of fledgling emancipative ideas set against a background of the political collapse of great empires and the emergence of successor states. These inchoate and newly-formed ideas received strong support in the pietist discourses of urban trading communities,[2] well before the encounter with Europe.

Ideally speaking, two major trends can be delineated among urban Muslims. On the one hand, we have established elites holding to a quasi-standard set of education and resources, with a trend toward centralized fiscal, administrative, and military polity, and standardization of the tax system. All this was designed as if to enable scribal groups to run the virtually independent provinces in the Mughal Empire. On the other hand, we find Muslim reformers challenging precisely this system, calling for processes of de-coupling from traditional norms and for religious individualization.

The first trend evolved around the set of knowledge known as *dars-e nizami,* a syllabus that supported Muslim scholastic philosophy and law. Its promoters combined the rational sciences—including philosophy—with mysticism, as represented by the Chishti-Qadiri orders. The second trend developed around new urban social formations who postulated a revival of transmitted sciences, that is, the Prophetic *hadîth,* Grounded in the puritan Naqshbandi order, these pietists called for Sufi reform and elaborated their ideas in the new linguistic medium, Urdu, with its multiple fora of articulation.[3]

The first tradition had its own dynamics, as it aimed at a policy of cultural integration in an area highly informed by shared traditions. I will focus, however, on discourses of the latter trend, the pietists, being well aware that the term has an origin in the study of Protestantism. Four issues will be dealt with: *Hadîth* studies, Sufi reform, literature, and public spaces.

The major concerns of Indian Muslim pietists were the criticism of what they saw as decadent mores, such as deviant shrine cultic practices and failing morality; advocacy of the unity between sacred and profane spheres, of the divine message and human practice; and the call to return to an original faith without sacerdotal authority.[4] This renewal of ethics and re-conversion, perceived as divine grace, was informed by the traditions of the Prophet Muhammad and the science of *hadîth* (literally, "the new," "news"), a trend also observed in other regions of the heterogeneous Islamic world, such as Egypt and Iran.[5] Centers for the circulation and exchange of such ideas were, among others, Mecca and Medina.[6]

The views were formulated in fledgling informal study circles combining *hadîth* studies with a social reformist agenda. *Hadîth* meetings were not new, but now their purview was expanded. Many of those who attended the study circles sought the separation of *hadîth* studies from the traditional scholarly establishment; the trimming of the chains of transmission; the reservation of *hadîth* as the exclusive domain of accepted traditionalists; the acquisition of authority by other scholars and common believers;[7] the space for acquiring critical and receptive competence; and the attainment and growth of cultural and social capital.

These study circles advocated appropriating God's message individually and independently by means of the revealed text. This appeal to *ijtihâd*[8] could be read as an expression of a desire for newness; it also implied emancipation from handed-down ties, something that harked back to the pious fathers in pristine Islam. The past referred to was not conceived as a heroic era that would recur, however. Rather, the past was experienced as a political and social utopia, which was to be recalled and translated into reality. Memory was transformed into powerful expectation;[9] recurrent rituals around the *hadîth* were proven devices to monumentalize this expectation. Needless to say, this sort of re-invention of tradition contrasted with the traditionally-bound compliance with law and authority, *taqlîd*. And *taqlîd* lived on in jurisprudence and philosophical theology, based on the rules and formal ideals of Aristotelian logic. This logic was, again, congruent with state domination.[10]

A famous representative of pietist ideas was Shâh Walî Ullâh (d. 1762), who considered *ijtihâd* an agent to establish coherence between the transmitted and the rational sciences,[11] as the rational sciences merely served to ascertain the authenticity of Sharia. In his endeavors Shâh Walî Ullâh was backed financially by emerging dynamic urban traders whose profit-thinking and credit-worthiness demanded moral behavior and Islamic legitimization.[12] Though little research has been done on this angle of his opinions, it seems that it was based in the "idea of performance with its revolutionary, anti-traditional explosive effect," as it opposed an "aristocratic patrician thinking of the privileged hierarchy established by birth-related estates."[13]

This process of emancipation promoted further arguments on various levels. Parallel to the renewed enthusiasm for *hadîth*, and the increasing recourse to *ijtihâd*, we find theoretical elaborations of the spiritual attitude of the so-called Muhammadan Path (*Tarîqa Muhammadîya*). For example, in "Lament of the Nightingale," the Naqshbandi mystic Nâsir 'Andalîb (d. 1758) argued for a radically internalized, inner worldly, ethical accountability of religion by means of the *khâlis* (true) Muhammadan Path.[14] In this ethical framework, which is still awaiting academic curiosity and attention, the handed-down trope of mystical annihilation in God was radically displaced by annihilation in the mystical master; "mystical piety" was replaced by "prophetic-" or "action-piety."[15] This *Fana fil Shaikh* did not, however, reproduce or aggravate hereditary loyalties toward established Shaikhs (pirism; Schimmel), a trend that had developed in the wake of Sufi intervention in the process of empire-building (1300-1700). On the contrary, quite in accord with the rise of *ijtihâd*, the trimming of the traditional chain of authorities (*isnad*) facilitated quick and effective affiliation with the Prophet Muhammad, the perfect man. The attribution of the human with divine characteristics anticipated the argument of later scholars, that God was able to create another Muhammad, the Seal of Prophets (*khatm al-anbiya*). This was contested by those who maintained that the creation of a peer of the Seal of Prophets was beyond even God's power.

In any case, this structural amnesia and invented genealogy rendered Uwais al-Qaranî and Khidr heroes. It would be worthwhile to know more about the Uwaisiyya and Khidariyya movements, both emerging in the 18th century and appealing to different social strata, in a time when multi-layered affiliations became quite popular.

The *Tariqa Muhammadiya*, in contrast, considered the *sunna* of the Prophet to be exemplary for social and political reform and called for a "Sunnatization" of life-worlds, indicating a subtle process of humanizing the Prophet and sanctifying the human. Shah Wali Ullah's complicated theoretical mystical constructions point to this development when he talks of levels of spirituality (*latâ'if*) achievable by man and "I-ness" in the sense of a universal identity (*ananîya*),[16] that is, the creation of exemplary individuals who would initiate the whole universe. Thus, practically experienced religion was reflected and conceptualized in abstract mystical theory. It is another matter that in 19th century, *Tariqa Muhammadiyya* developed into hierarchically structured mass organizations in various regional settings.

Doubts and skepticism were important presuppositions for an emerging consciousness of human equality; these were expressed in various spheres of culture, such as music and its theoretical elaborations.[17] We know, for example, that during the reign of Muhammad Shâh (1719-1748) *khayâl* (literally, "idea," "imagination") and *qawwâlî*, mystical poems, ousted the classical, statutory *dhrupad. Khayâl* and mystical singing acknowledged individual improvisation and technical virtuosity, and were cultivated in musical gatherings,[18] a field that has been looked into only recently.

Other traces of individuation and personal ostentation can be found in the new literary medium, Urdu, championed by members of the relatively sober Naqshbandiyya.[19] This language accommodated and celebrated newness, abandoning teleological God-centeredness in favor of self-conscious and free-acting awareness; it expressed emancipation from prestigious cultural languages like the canonical, rigid, Arabic as well as the refined, subtle, Persian.[20]

Thus, the literary critic Ahmad Ali later wrote both of the cultural upheaval of the time and the great daring of those poets who chose to write in Urdu:

> ...the removal of restrictions placed on the mind, and the release of the imagination from the imposed religious beliefs rooted in orthodoxy... led to a revival of the arts and mysticism, and the awakening of a critical spirit which refused to take things on mere authority..."[21]

> ...it is the final choice of Urdu that marks the beginning and flowering of... the emancipation of the mind from the darkness of didacticism and crude expression.[22]

Indeed, poets like Mir Taqî Mîr (d. 1810) conjured, with his apocalyptic verses, the beginning of a new era that questioned the social situation of impoverishment and depression in post-Mughal Delhi.[23] Terms like "breach" and "defeat," "loss" and "alienation" (*shekast, qafas, wahshat, zulm, faryâd*) were celebrated.[24] The Naqshbandi Mîr Dard (d. 1785) reflected on his *weltschmerz* in the face of political decline; he also traced the pains involved in his process of individuation. Some principles of the Naqshbandiyya such as *safar dar watan*—the "journey to the homeland" (or "journey to/in the soul," or "journey to/in the Self")—and the calm devotional act of the *dhikr*—the inner recollection of God—may have been vehicles in his process of self-discovery and introjection.[25] To him poetry was "an expression of recent experiences that shook the poet's heart, phrasing one's innermost feelings (*wâridât-e qalbîyah*) and experiences in a way that the verses deeply dug into in the listeners' hearts."[26] Mîr Dard, thus, elevated tenderness to a leitmotif that combined sensuality with virtue and rationality. Perhaps this sort of poetry conveyed inwardness based on subjective perceptions and their spiritual digestion. The genre of *shahr-âshûb*[27] ("the shattered city") was also a proven "medium of expression for feelings of sensitive human beings (*hassâs insân*),"[28] especially as it distinguished along societal formations. Unfortunately for those of us in South Asian Studies, to date no scholar has approached these texts in this fashion, or looked into this sort of reading.

Furthermore, as Jamil Jalibi[29] has it, Mîr Taqî Mîr wrote,

> autobiographical stories (*apnî dhât kî hikâyat*) ...comparable to introspective studies (*khûd mutâla'ah*). Indeed, Mîr's protagonists did not represent kings, ministers, and princes or princesses but simple people who were scared (*wâlhânah-pan*) and self-critical (*khûd-sapurd-agî*)... and who presented their lives open and above board, with all sorrows and fears...

Increasingly during this period, references to personal impressions and emotions can be accounted for, demanding change in the social and ontological orders. Similar features can be traced in other parts of the Islamic world, such as in Cairo, where "the poet wrote about his own feelings with obvious sincerity."[30]

By analogy, childhood at this time emerged as a distinctly significant part of human life. Just recall the revealing passages in Mîr Taqî Mîr's autobiography, when he talks with his nurse and his father, or remembers his father's affectionate ways with him.[31] In the European context this certainly underpins the emergence of individualism and sensitive human beings (*hassâs insân*). One wonders whether new stylistic ideals corresponded to a cult of emotions, and when immediacy and naturalness were passionately debated and made a topic of discourse. This emotional differentiation and inner experience—in short, sensitivity, a spiritual trend of the 18th century—was perceived by sensitive people as achieving equality in action and emotion.[32]

It seems that politically conscious men were eager to take their destiny into their own hands. Therefore poets approved of the right to resist established authorities. These ideas required an experiential space of sensitivity in order to acquire new social significance, a place where economic, social, and cultural capital was transmitted, nurturing ideals such as sociability and communality. Such a space was the *mushâ'irah*, a literary salon with poetry competitions.[33] Similar tendencies can be discerned in other regions of the Orient when "the revival of these studies (e.g., *hadîth*) among [sufi] reformers turned their *majlis* into a religio-cultural institution, a literary salon."[34]

The Naqshbandi Mîr Dard is considered the first poet to restore the popularity of the *mushâ'irah*.[35] In his "place of sitting," participation went well beyond "a middle class interested in Persian and Urdu poetry and literature and among whom one could count representatives of the military and administration as well as notables and traders."[36] The *Musha'ira* also allowed a larger public, by providing a gregarious forum for communication. It offered a constant co-option of new members from the lower classes, including barbers, soldiers, perfume vendors, masons, weavers, tailors, and carpenters.[37] Such a process certainly facilitated new experiences and social openness. The equal status of the attendees within this egalitarian arena provided a locus for cross-class dialogue along with a new level of interpersonal relationships and personal disclosure. This gave rise to a new trend in taste; it also formed a moral institution that helped highlight essential ideas, specifying the contexts of activity and awarding them validity—an anti-space to the court, as it were.

These gatherings did have their habitual guidelines (*âdâb*), but they intentionally ignored religion and politics. Emotion, sensitivity, individuality, and personality development were of prime concern. And the emphasis on self-definition and self-discovery invited the articulation of one's individual deficiencies, which were now appreciated as individually-accountable human weaknesses.

These spaces were, by their very public nature, also very visible. They existed in areas open to the public, such as libraries, coffeehouses, and baths,[38] the number of which increased rapidly during this period. It is no wonder, then, that contemporary Indian travelers to Europe were able to perceive similar institutions there within their own cultural paradigms.[39] Hardly anybody has enquired into this aspect of material culture, however.

Similarly, a closer identification between master and pupil emerged (another subject that deserves to be explored further).[40] Within the learning process, the master endowed the student with a *nom de plume* (*takhallus*: "becoming free," "liberation").[41] This metamorphosis created distance from the self, suggesting a new, albeit temporary, identity. Within this liminal space, this transitional, artificial person (*takhallus*) is free to abandon society, and is suspended "betwixt and between" social categories. Translating *takhallasa min* thus, as disembbeding from established loyalties and received traditions (*taqlîd*),[42] signifies finding, observing, and constructing the subject anew.

When 'Andalîb talked about the process of self-discovery, he found that, on his way to cognition, he had broken the mirror.[43] Mîr Taqî Mîr agreed: "It is man, who inspires the world with life! A mirror though it was, no doubt, before man existed—but a mirror unable to allow for the Vision."[44] And Dard exclaimed: "Throughout life I have been listening to Him from afar / Only in the state of dreaming I dragged Him to my breast / Now, as I presented myself as a mirror in front of Him / He saw himself, not I saw Him."[45]

Whether this interpretation of *takhallus* can also be read in terms of Dumont's individual-outside-the-world, i.e., the Indian renouncer—who in fact becomes the dynamic center of religious development and change in contrast to the man-in-the-world—is another area yet to be explored.

The *Mushâ'irah* as a means of self-liberation advanced institutionalized literary criticism, in the form of memoirs, biographies, and autobiographies. Anthologies of poetry and biographical collections extending beyond classical hagiographies, as well as lexicons and encyclopedia, became popular. The three earliest (Persian) biographies of Urdu poets were written between 1752 and 1754.[46] Such endeavors signify contemporary aspirations to intellectual universality and a desire to summarize and popularize the accumulated knowledge systematically.[47]

This emancipatory approach can be related to the economic and social interests of an aspiring trading community who considered morality, virtue, and equality to be important. They looked for credit-worthiness and the organized control of capital, which was opposed to the gentry's unprofessional conduct and their exploitation of their status-related wealth and opulence. The value of individuals competed with the value of status. Functionality, too, contrasted with enjoyment; common, untitled property was earned by hard work, and did not consist of secured landed property. Rather, it was made up of monetary and commodity assets, which, if they were to increase, had to be invested at risk, again and again. The commoner was eager to acquire and maintain wealth; the aristocrat was fixated on its waste and application.[48] Obviously, both trends constituted a force-field within which other actors played out the roles of other dimensions.

To conclude, I offer that pietist ideas and the reinforcement of *ijtihad* seemed to initiate self-reflexivity and individualization, with the Prophetic *sunna* being the point of reference for social and political reform. Religion experienced practically was reflected in abstract concepts; the sacred was humanized, and the human was sacralized. All of this can be seen in the writings of the age, works such as pietistic texts and poetry circulated widely in the bazaar. The visibility of publicly accessible spaces which afforded intermingling between various social strata, such as poetry meetings and other institutions, significantly aided several endeavors to achieve emancipation. Do we know of any parallels to this movement in the Hindu context?

Interestingly, these ideas soon attracted colonialists as well, who at times even indulged in cultural mimicry. But this process threatened the the very nature of the colonial project. Therefore, the semantics of traditionalization and, following that, of modernization of the Orient through the colonizing mission was to endow the colony with "civility" in order to safeguard its economic exploitation.

Thus the initial process of emancipation in the 18th century was radicalized in the 19th century. One may consider the following phase in terms of neo-confessionalism, characterized by a high degree of diffusion of Islamic learning and piety, facilitated through media, increasing mobility throughout the Muslim world, and pan-Islamic sentiments. Islamic puritanism played an important and expanding role, because it appeared in different—sometimes contradictory—forms, such as scripturalist yet sufic. The latter was integral to society and prominent even as urban reformist movements were trying to get rid of it. The revival of ritual activities and scriptural norms were important in establishing distinct contesting confessional groups, in the public sphere. These groups were later complemented by yet others during the anti-colonial struggle.

Notes

1. This is a shorter and slightly modified version of my "Muslim Culture and Reform in 18th Century South Asia." *Journal of the Royal Asiatic Society* 13.2 (2003): 227-243.

2. For indigenous presuppositions of the world market in South Asia see David Washbrook, "Progress and Problems: South Asian Social and Economic History, c. 1720-1860" in *Modern Asian Studies* 22 (1988): 57-96; David Washbrook, "South Asia, The World System, and World Capitalism" in *Journal of Asian Studies* 49.3 (1990): 479-508; C.A. Bayly, *Indian Society and the Making of the British Empire The New Cambridge History of India, II.1.* Cambridge, 1990, esp. Chapter I; and K.N. Chaudhuri, *Trade and Civilization in the Indian Ocean: An Economic History from the Rise of Islam to 1750.* Cambridge, 1985: 221. For the development of a world economy as a marker for the distinction of the early modern period, see Ferdnand Braudel, *Sozialgeschichte des 15-18 Jahrhunderts: Aufbruch zur Weltwirtschaft.* München: Der Handel, 1990.

3. For details, see Jamal Malik, *Islamische Gelehrtenkultur in Nordindien. Entwicklungsgeschichte und Tendenzen am Beispiel von Lucknow.* Leiden, 1997.

4. These and the reforms which follow them have much in common with the Christian pietist movements in the Protestant church that began in the last quarter of the 17th century. See *Pia Desideria,* by Jakob Philipp Spener (1635-1705).

5. Algar, Hamid: "Shi'ism and Iran in the Eighteenth

Century" in *Studies in Eighteenth-Century Islamic History*. Thomas Naff and Roger Owen, eds. Carbondale, IL: Southern Illinois UP, 1977: 288-302; Mangol Bayat and Ahmad Kazemi Moussavi, "The Usuli-Akhbari Controversy" in *Expectation of the Millennium: Shi'ism in History*. S.H. Nasr, ed. Albany: State U of New York P, 1989: 281-286; Etan Kohlberg, "Aspects of Akhbari Thought in the Seventeenth and Eighteenth Centuries" in *Eighteenth Century Renewal and Reform in Islam.* Nehemia Levtzion and John O. Voll, eds. Syracuse, NY: Syracuse UP, 1987: 133-160.

6. See N. Levtzion and John O. Voll, eds., *Eighteenth-Century Renewal and Reform in Islam.* Syracuse, NY: Syracuse UP, 1987.

7. Similarly in other Muslim regions; see John Voll, *Islam: Continuity and Change in the Modern World.* Boulder, CO: Westview Press, 1982, pp. 72-ff; Peter Gran, *Islamic Roots of Capitalism: Egypt, 1760-1840.* Austin, TX: U of Texas P, 1979. pp. 49-ff, 112, 139.

8. Compare Rudolph Peters, "Idjtihad and Taqlid in 18th and 19th Century Islam," in *Die Welt des Islams* 20 (1980), pp. 131-145. See also Wael B. Hallaq, "Was the Gate of Ijtihad Closed?" in *International Journal for Middle East Studies* 16 (1984), pp. 3-41.

9. Jan Assmann, *Das Kulturelle Gedächtnis: Schrift, Erinnerung und Politische Identität in Frühen Hochkulturen.* München: Beck, 1992. p. 80.

10. "kalam was most congruent with state domination..." Peter Gran, *Islamic Roots of Capitalism: Egypt, 1760-1840.* Austin, TX: U of Texas P, 1979 pp. xvi, f. 50, 96.

11. For Shâh Walî Ullâh's *ijtihâd*-concept see Daud Rahbar, 'Shah Waliullah and Ijtihad: Translation of Selected Passages from his 'Iqd al-Jid fi Ahkam al-Ijtihad wa'l-Taqlid'" in *The Muslim World* 45.4 (1955): 346-

358.

12. Shâh Walî Ullâh, *Tafhîmât-e Illâhîya*, 2 Vols., Ghûlâm Mustafâ al-Qâsimî, ed. Ḥaydarābād: Akādīmīyat al-Shāh Walī Allāh al-Dihlawī, 1967-1970. Vol. I. pp. 282-288.

13. Hans-Ulrich Wehler, *Aus der Geschichte Lernen?* München, Beck, 1988. p. 222.

14. Nâsir 'Andalîb, *Nâla-ye 'Andalîb*, 2 Vols. Rpt. Bhopāl: Maṭba' Shāhjahānī, 1890. Originally this was delivered in Hindustani and, at the wishes of his followers, was written down in Persian. For Nâsir 'Andalîb see Annemarie Schimmel, *Pain and Grace: A Study of Two Mystical Writers of Eighteenth-Century Muslim India.* Leiden: Brill, 1976. pp. 32-ff *et passim*; S.A.A. Rizvi, *Shâh Walî Allâh and His Time.* Canberra: Ma'rifat, 1980. pp. 343-ff; S. 'Abd al-Hayy, *Nuzhat al-khawâtir wa bahjat al-masâmi' wa al-nawâzir, I-VIII*, compiled and edited by S. al-Dīn Aḥmad and Abū al-Ḥasan 'Alī al-Ḥasanī al-Nadwī. Ḥaydarābād: Dā'irat al-Ma'ārif, 1947-1956. VI, pp. 368f.

15. See Annemarie Schimmel, *Mystische Dimensionen Des Islam.* Aalen: Qualandar Verlag, 1979. pp. 288-ff.

16. See Shâh Walî Ullâh, *Tafhîmât-e Illâhîya*, 2 Vols., Ghûlâm Mustafâ al-Qâsimî, ed. Ḥaydarābād: Akādīmīyat al-Shāh Walī Allāh al-Dihlawī, 1967-1970. I, pp. 229-ff; Marcia Hermansen, "Shâh Walî Allâh's Theory of the Subtle Spiritual Centers (*latâ'if*): A Sufi Model of Personhood and Self-Transformation" in *Journal of Near Eastern Studies* 47 (1988): 1-25.

17. See Dargah-Quli Khan, *Maraqqa'-e-Dehli: The Mugal Capital in Muhammad Shah's Time.* Delhi: Deputy Publ, 1989. pp. xxxii-ff.

18. Dargah-Quli Khan, *Maraqqa'-e-Dehli: The Mugal Capital in Muhammad Shah's Time.* Delhi: Deputy Publ, 1989. pp. 75-ff, 113. On his journey to Delhi he con-

sidered *dhrupad*-interpreters outdated; he opined that *khayâl* and *qawwâlî* were *en vogue*; see also N.A. Jairazbhoy, *The Rāgs of North Indian Music: Their Structure and Evolution*. London: Faber and Faber, 1971. pp. 18-21; Najma P. Ahmad, *Hindustani Music: A Study of Its Development in Seventeenth and Eighteenth Centuries*. New Delhi: Manohar, 1984. Introduction.

19. "One of the surprises in Indian cultural history around 1700 is, that members of the 'anti-artistic' Naqshbandiyya order were instrumental in the development of a new literary medium which was, after Aurangzeb's death, to supersede Persian and to become the typical language of Indian Muslims: that is Urdu." See Annemarie Schimmel, *Pain and Grace: A Study of Two Mystical Writers of Eighteenth-Century Muslim India*. Leiden: Brill, 1976. p. 11. Naqshbandis were also most prominent in the expansion of Urdu prose; see Muḥammad A Qādrī, *Urdū Nas̱r Ke Irtiqā' Meṉ 'ulamā' Kā Ḥiṣṣah: Shamālī Hind Meṉ 1857 Tak*. Lāhore: Idārah-yi S̱aqāfat-i Islāmiyyah, 1988; 'Abd al-Haqq, *Urdû kî ibtedâ'î nashû o numâ men sûfîyâ'-ye karâm kâ kâm*. New Delhi: n.p., 1988; B. Rihânah Fârûqî, *Dehlî ke mashâ'ikh kî adabî khidmât*. Delhi: 1988.

20. For the history and development of Urdu literature see Jamil Jâlibî, *Tarikh-e-adab-e-urdu*. Delhi: Educational Press, 1984; Muhammad Husain Azâd, *Ab-i Hayat: Yani Mashahir Shura-Yi Urdu Ke Savanih Umri Aur Zaban-I Mazkur Ki Ahd Ba Ahd Ki Taraqqiyon Aur Islahon Ka Bayan*. Lāhaur: Maṭba'-i Mufīd-i 'Ām, 1907; Hakîm S. 'Abd al- Hayy, *Gul-e Ra'nâ'*. Azamgarh: 1923; Ursula Rothen-Dubs, ed., *Allahs Indischer Garten: Ein Lesebuch Der Urdu-Literatur*. Frauenfeld: Waldgut, 1989; Muhammad Sadiq, *A History of Urdu Literature*. London: Oxford UP, 1984; R.B. Saksena, *A History of Urdu Literature*. Lahore: Sind Sagar Academy, 1975; Annemarie

Schimmel, *Classical Urdu Literature from the Beginning to Iqbāl.* Wiesbaden: Harrassowitz, 1975; C. Shackle, ed., *Urdu in Muslim South Asia; Studies in the Honour of Ralph Russell.* London, School of Oriental and African Studies, University of London, 1989; D.J. Matthews and C. Shackle, eds., *An Anthology of Classical Urdu Love Lyrics, Text and Translations.* London: Oxford UP, 1972; M. Garcin de Tassy, *Histoire de la Littérature Hindouie et Hindoustani, I-III* rep. New York: B. Franklin, 1968; 'Alî Jawwâd Zaidî, *Do Adabī Iskūl: Nihād-i Lakhn'au Aur Dilī Iskūlon̲ Ke Mushtarak K̲h̲aṣūṣiyāt.* Lakhn'au: Nasīm buk ḍipo, 1970.

21. Ahmad Ali, *The Golden Tradition.* NY: Columbia UP, 1973. p. 73.

22. Ahmad Ali, *The Golden Tradition.* NY: Columbia UP, 1973. pp. 23-ff.

23. Such as: "This age is not like that which went before. The times have changed, the earth and sky have changed." Or, "Wherever you look, a poem full of apocalyptic sound appears; Everywhere in my works is found, A tumult like the Day of Doom." Mîr Taqî Mîr as quoted in Ahmad Ali, *The Golden Tradition.* NY: Columbia UP, 1973. pp. 23-25.

24. Compare Jamil Jâlibî, *Tarikh-e-adab-e-urdu.* Delhi: Educational Press, 1984. Vol II, pp. 492-ff.

25. For Dard the questioning of his own identity was in fact crucial (see Annemarie Schimmel, *Pain and Grace: A Study of Two Mystical Writers of Eighteenth-Century Muslim India.* Leiden: Brill, 1976. pp. 41, 84-ff, 97-ff). Accordingly he was of the view that while man was created to feel the pain of (mystical) love, angels were merely obedient to God (see Annemarie Schimmel, *Mystische Dimensionen Des Islam.* Aalen: Qualandar Verlag, 1979, p. 532).

26. Jamil Jâlibî, *Tarikh-e-adab-e-urdu.* Delhi: Educa-

tional Press, 1984. Vol. II, p. 472.

27. See Muhammad Sadiq, *A History of Urdu Literature.* London: Oxford UP, 1984. pp. 117-ff.

28. Jamil Jâlibî, *Tarikh-e-adab-e-urdu.* Delhi: Educational Press, 1984. Vol. II, p. 484.

29. Jamil Jâlibî, *Tarikh-e-adab-e-urdu.* Delhi: Educational Press, 1984. Vol. II, p. 476, p. 631.

30. Peter Gran, *Islamic Roots of Capitalism: Egypt, 1760-1840.* Austin, TX: U of Texas P, 1979. p. 57.

31. C.M. Naim, ed. and transl., *Zikr-i Mir: The Autobiography of the Eighteenth-Century Mughal Poet Mir Muhammad Taqi "Mir" (1723-1810).* New Delhi: Oxford UP, 1999.

32. For the literary expansion of sensitivity in a European context see Klaus P. Hansen, *Kultur und Kulturwissenschaft: Eine Einführung.* Tübingen u.a: Francke, 1995. pp. 98-ff; also Klaus P. Hansen, ed., *Empfindsamkeiten,* Passau: Wissesnchaftsverlag R. Rothe, 1990.

33. For this see C.M. Naim, "Poet-Audience Interaction at Urdu *musha'iras,*" in C. Shackle, ed., *Urdu in Muslim South Asia; Studies in the Honour of Ralph Russell.* London, School of Oriental and African Studies, University of London, 1989. pp. 167-173; 'Alî Jawwâd Zaidî, *Târîkh-e mushâ'irah.* Delhi: 1989; Brian Q. Silver, "The Urdu *Mushâ'irah,*" in Alma Giese and J. Christoph Bürgel, eds., *Gott Ist Schön Und Er Liebt Die Schönheit: Festschrift Für Annemarie Schimmel Zum 7. April 1992, Dargebracht Von Schülern, Freunden Und Kollegen.* Bern: Peter Lang, 1994. pp. 363-375; Farhatullah Baig, *The Last Musha'irah of Dehli: A Translation into English of Farhatullah Baig's Modern Urdu Classic, Delhi Ki Akhri Shama' ; with an Introduction, Notes, Glossary, and Bibliography.* New Delhi: Orient Longman, 1979. An academic work on this complex issue of *mushâ'ira* as a cultural and social institution has still to be written.

34. Peter Gran, *Islamic Roots of Capitalism: Egypt, 1760-1840.* Austin, TX: U of Texas P, 1979. pp. 57-ff.

35. "It seems that the institution of *mushâ'ira*... was developed during Dard's lifetime." Annemarie Schimmel, *Classical Urdu Literature from the Beginning to Iqbāl*. Wiesbaden: Harrassowitz, 1975. p. 171; Zaidî, *Mushâ'irah*, pp. 75-ff.

36. 'Alî Jawwâd Zaidî, *Târîkh-e mushâ'irah*. Delhi: 1989. pp. 109-ff.

37. Compare Mohammad Umar, "Literature of a Declining Empire: Urdu Poetry in the Eighteenth Century," presented at the 52nd Session of the Indian History Congress, New Delhi, 1992.

38. For coffee-houses, see for example Dargah-Quli Khan, *Maraqqa'-e-Delhi: The Mugal Capital in Muhammad Shah's Time*. Delhi: Deputy Publ, 1989. pp. 25, *et passim*.

39. See the reciprocal perception in the case of Mîrzâ Abû Tâlib Khân Isfahânî, *Masīr-i Ṭālibī, Yā, Safar'nāmah-'i Mīrzā Abū Ṭālib Khān*. Rpt. ed. Tihran: Shirkat-i Sahāmī-i Kitābhā-yi Jībī, 1974. pp. 181-ff, 303-ff, 355-ff; C. Stewart, trans., *The Travels of Mirza Abu Taleb Khan, in Asia, Africa, and Europe, During the Years 1799, 1800, 1801, 1802, and 1803*. 2 vols. London, 1810; Michael Fisher, ed., *The Travels of Dean Mahomet: An Eighteenth-Century Journey Through India*. Berkeley: U of California P, 1997; S. Digby, "An Eighteenth Century Narrative of a Journey from Bengal to England: Munshî Ismâ'îl's *New History,*" in C. Shackle, ed., *Urdu in Muslim South Asia; Studies in the Honour of Ralph Russell*. London, School of Oriental and African Studies, University of London, 1989. pp. 49-66; Shaikh Lutfullah, *Autobiography of Lutfullah: An Indian's Perceptions of the West*. Rpt. ed. Edward B. Eastwick, ed., with an Introduction by S.A.I. Tirmizi. New Delhi: International Writers' Emporium, 1985; Reinhard Schulze,

"Schauspiel oder Nachahmung? Zum Theaterbegriff arabischer Reiseschriftsteller im 19. Jahrhundert," *Die Welt des Islams* 34 (1994): pp. 67-84.

40. C.M. Naim, "Poet-Audience Interaction at Urdu *Musha'iras,*" in C. Shackle, ed., *Urdu in Muslim South Asia; Studies in the Honour of Ralph Russell.* London, School of Oriental and African Studies, University of London, 1989. p. 173; ‚Alî Jawwâd Zaidî, *Târîkh-e mushâ'irah.* Delhi: 1989. pp. 151-ff.

41. See ‚Alî Jawwâd Zaidî, *Târîkh-e mushâ'irah.* Delhi: 1989. pp. 170-185; Annemarie Schimmel, *Classical Urdu Literature from the Beginning to Iqbāl.* Wiesbaden: Harrassowitz, 1975. p. 174; Ralph Russell and Khvurshīdulislām. *Three Mughal Poets: Mir, Sauda, Mir Hasan.* Cambridge, MA: Harvard UP, 1968. pp. 3-ff.

42. The well-known lexicographer S. Muhammad Mîrzâ Muhadhdhab, in *Muhadhdhab al-Lughât,* (Lucknow, n.p.) Vol. 3, p. 240, prefers a different—albeit not very inspiring and conventional—explanation: *takhallus* (ending) is used because the poetry ends with the pseudonym.

43. See Nâsir 'Andalîb, *Nâla-ye 'Andalîb,* 2 Vols. Rpt. Bhopāl: Maṭba' Shāhjahānī, 1890. I, p. 790.

44. As quoted in Ursula Rothen-Dubs, ed., *Allahs Indischer Garten: Ein Lesebuch Der Urdu-Literatur.* Frauenfeld: Waldgut, 1989. p. 20 (my translation).

45. Quoted in Annemarie Schimmel, *Liebe Zu Dem Einen: Texte Aus Der Mystischen Tradition Des Indischen Islam.* Zürich: Benziger, 1986. p. 124 (my translation).

46. Mîr Taqî Mîr, *Nikāt Al-Shu'arā: Ya'nī, Tazkira-I Shu'arā-I Urdu: Points or Conciets of the Poets; I.e., Biographical Memoirs of Urdu Poets.* Badayut: Nizami Press, 1900; 'Alī, al-Ḥusainī Gardezî and K. Akbar Ḥaidarī, *Tazkirah-yi Rekhtah Goyān.* Lakhna'ū: Uttar Pradesh Urdū Akādmī, 1995; Muhammad Qiyamud-Din Qâ´im

Chândpûrî, *Makhzan-e Nikât, A Biographical Anthology of Early Poets, Compiled in 1755*. Rpt. Lahore: The Board of Advancement of Literature, 1966; compare Farmân Fatehpûrî, *Urdû Shu'arâ ke Radhkire awr Tadhkirah Nigârî*. Lahore: Majlas-i-Tarraqi-i-Adab, 1972; Jamil Jâlibî, *Tarikh-e-adab-e-urdu*. Delhi: Educational Press, 1984. II, pp. 496-ff.

47. Compare Urs Bitterli, *Die Wilden und die Zivilisierten: Grundzüge einer Geistes- und Kulturgeschichte der europäisch-überseeischen Begegnung*. München: Verl. C. H. Beck, 1991. p. 223.

48. Klaus P. Hansen, "Bürgerliche und Unbürgerliche Empfindsamkeit in England," in Klaus P. Hansen, ed., *Empfindsamkeiten*, Passau: Wissesnchaftsverlag R. Rothe, 1990. pp. 43-62, here p. 50.

Dr. Jamal Malik is a Professor of Islamic Studies and chair of Religious Studies – Islamic Studies at the University of Erfurt, Germany.

CHAPTER 7

A.L. SAFRONOVA

The Past and Present of Theravada Buddhism in Sri Lanka: Traditional Heritage v. the Challenge of Modernity

The 20th century was a period of intensive research on Buddhism both in the East and the West. Buddhological studies have a long history, but real academic research started in the late 19th century, when the emphasis on ancient Indian studies in general, and Sanskrit studies in particular, were based mainly on the Mahayana texts, which offered more material for deep philosophical research than for historical interpretation. Gradually academic interest shifted to the studies of Pali texts, as well as Buddhist chronology.

Studies in South Asian Theravada tradition open the field for a historical research, as this very tradition produces brilliant example of early historical thinking which was crystallized in Buddhist sources. Buddhist chronicles such as *Mahavamsa, Dipavamsa, Culavamsa, Rajavaliya, Pujavaliya, Rajaratnakaraya,*

Nikaya-samgrahaya, Mahabodhivamsa, Thupavamsa, Dathavamsa and others,[1] created in Lanka, became an important historical source for South Asia as a whole.

Buddhist chronicles are not just a part of the historical heritage, the tradition is alive—a special Council of Mahatheras was established in Sri Lanka in 1956, the year which was celebrated as the 2500th anniversary of Buddha's parinirvana, to continue Mahavamsa.[2]

The Buddhist historiographical tradition was born in the 4th and 5th centuries CE on the island of Lanka, which was destined to become a cradle of Theravada Buddhism in South Asia, beginning in the 3rd century BCE. On this island, *Tipitaka,* the Buddhist canon, was written down in the 1st century BCE. Thus, in the mind of a Buddhist devotee, Lanka bears high status as *Dhammadipa/Dharmadvipa* or *Buddhadipa/Buddhadvipa*, an island-custodian of the Word of Buddha. After independence, Sri Lanka declared itself a Buddhist state, and still follows this goal despite changes in its political, social, and economic spheres.[3]

The main aim of this article is to show the continuity of the Theravada tradition as it is preserved in modern Sri Lanka (while in its motherland, India, it came close to pure extinction), and to focus on those features and sides of monastic life and organization of *sangha* which were maintained through the ages despite the process of structural segmentation and conceptual differentiation of Buddhist *sangha* in Sri Lanka. There are over 20 *nikayas* today, with three mainstream divisions: *Siam-nikaya, Amarapura-nikaya,* and *Ramannya-nikaya.*[4] Contradictions and discrepancies in understanding the nature of *nikaya* formation in Sri Lankan Buddhism are numerous.[5] Some of the questions raised in the discussions seem to be categorized as "eternal."

What is the difference between the Indian and Sri Lankan scenarios in the fate and historical ways of the development of Buddhism? What is the nature and origin of Buddhist decline, or, on the other hand, revival? What was the background for the flourishing of Theravada in Lanka, while in India it was supplanted by Mahayana schools, and then by Hinduism?

Shall we consider the split of *sangha* into different *nikayas* as a sign of decline, and its unification as a manifestation of the revival of the order? Can we look at the history of Buddhist *sangha* in terms of periodically changing cycles of revival and decline? Which correlation between Tradition and Reform created an optimal climate for the promotion of the welfare of Buddhist institutions?

The prominence and significance of Buddhism in Sri Lanka and the vitality of Buddhist tradition in all periods of its history was maintained due to the dominance of *sangha* and Buddhist ideological institutions in the social and cultural life of the country. Buddhist civilization preserved itself in the face of the calamities of history in South Asia and in India itself, and managed not only to survive but to strengthen itself, overcoming its initial historical and geographical boundaries. This became possible due to the coexistence of two tendencies both immanent to the Buddhist tradition: the evolutionary, reformative, character of this religion coupled with its extraordinary capability to preserve its purity, despite the impact of changing political situations, including the withdrawal of state patronage.[6]

The process of structural segmentation and conceptual differentiation in the Buddhist *sangha* of Sri Lanka was constant through the ages, but the complexity of reasons and the particular mechanisms of *nikaya* formation were different. They were caused by many factors among which the interrelation between *sangha* and state was the most important. The main feature in the development of Theravada is the continuity of Buddhist tradition in medieval, colonial, and modern Sri Lanka, despite the withdrawal of state patronage during four and half centuries of European dominance on the island.[7]

The political changes in Sinhalese society and the developments within the *sangha* were closely connected, and the periods of constructive reforms of Buddhism, the unification and purification of *sangha*, usually fell during periods of political centralization, while the periods of distributed polity led to fragmentation of the Order, but this interdependency didn't work without exceptions.[8]

In traditional pre-colonial society the links between *sangha* and state were firm, and both organizational models and the modes of *bhikkhu* behavior were in concordance with the needs of society, though this rule was spread only in the official hierarchy of the *sangha*. A dispersed system of monasteries, schools, and trends was obviously free from central state control and existed autonomously all over the country. *Sangha* included both support of the state and opposition to the state. Part of it was entirely out of politics.

Organizational models, varying between the poles of extravertiveness—*gamavasi, nagaravasi bhikkhu*, and intravertiveness—*vanavasi bhikkhu*, the corresponding ritual and behavioral stereotypes of Buddhist monks, social and caste composition, and geographical localization of monasteries, and the interpretation of the Buddhist canon were, thus, very different. The amorphous, loose, and unstable structure of society—with periods of social, economic, ethnic, and confessional formation—stimulated the endless process of differentiation and reorganization, and formed the reformative strife within the *sangha*.

Sangha was not united since the early Anuradhapura period. The chronicles depict the rivalry between *Mahavihara, Abhayagirivihara* and *Jetavanaramavihara,* and among the smaller sectarian groups as well. In the Polonnaruwa period, *sangha* was said to be constructed of eight fraternities. The crucial period of the 13th and 14th centuries, marked by the decline of the states of the Northeastern "dry zone" and the shift of political and religio-cultural centers within the island to the central areas and to the "wet zone" of the Southwest, caused structural changes in the society and its socio-economic institutions which in turn had their effects on the state of the Buddhist *sangha*. The split of the state led to the further fragmentation of *sangha* and the appearance of new fraternities striving for structural reform and conceptual differentiation.[9]

If the monasteries and schools of the previous periods were rivals in seeking the patronage and recognition of one center of power (Anuradhapura from the 3rd century BCE to the 10th century CE; then Polonnaruwa from the 11th century CE to the 13th century CE), now, when the monarch was no longer one, the situation became much more complicated. Decentralization of the state led to the formation of *nikayas* which associated themselves with different centers of power (Dambadeniya, Gampola, Yapahuwa, Kurunegala, etc.) and rival *nikayas* within each particular state as well. This combined with further fragmentation of the Order on a caste and ethnicity basis. Various *nikayas* began their separate existence within the frame of several patronizing forces, and their positions differed greatly by the time of the establishment of Kotte, Sitavaka, Rayigama and Kandy as new centers of power.

The 13th and 14th centuries were a period not only of internal migrations, but of external as well; the extreme frequency of such from various parts of the Indian subcontinent obviously changed both the society and *sangha*. Some groups of Indian migrants were Buddhists (by that time Buddhism was in decline in India), some adopted this religion and incorporated themselves into the structure of Sinhalese Buddhist society, forming a number of castes, seeking for their representation within the *sangha* and thus increasing its heterogeneity. Adoption of Sinhalese as a mother tongue and the practice of intermarrying led to the widening of the meaning "Sinhalese," which became more of a cultural and political identification, rather than ethnic in the strict sense of the term. Religion, thus, becomes the central focus of identity and the striving for unification of the *sangha* receives one more dimension: it becomes closely connected to the formation not only of one state but one ethnicity.

An ethnically plural society developed a syncretic type of self-identification, and Buddhism appeared as a system which cemented a socium composed of immensely different populations. Historical and ethnic consciousness of Sinhala was obviously formed through Buddhist categories, which is proved by the appearance of the Buddhist chronicle tradition not only in Pali, but in the Sinhalese language as well (13th century CE). Ethnic consolidation led to the incorporation of non-Buddhist deities into the Buddhist pantheon, and the growing syncretism of Buddhism created a background for further segmentation of the *sangha*.[10]

The meaning of the term *dussila bhikkhu*, thus, becomes more complicated. According to early chronicles, *dussila bhikkhu*, or *adhammavadino bhikkhu*, or *alajji bhikkhu*, or *bhedakara bhikkhu*, means a monk who failed to follow the formulations of Vinaya and didn't obey the rules of the established *nikaya*. *Dambadeni-katikavata* (13th century, the reign of Parakramabahu II) gave a new dimension to the term, prohibiting the grant of *pabbajja* to individuals of low castes, obviously belonging to the newly-forming stratum of Sinhalese society, and proclaiming admittance to *sangha* only for *Kulinas*, the elite castes, as a preventive measure from the newcomers.

This practice existed for centuries, and it is seems that the only period when it was neglected for a short time was during the period of Buddhist reformer Valivita Saranankara's activities in the last quarter of the 18th century, after which it was again announced by the newly-formed *Siam Nikaya* on the verge of the 19th century.[11]

The *Sasana Katikavatas*, the royal edicts, reveal the attempts of the kings in power and the *sangha* rajas to reorganize *sangha* and to introduce new rules and restrictions due to the practical needs of the period, because the Vinaya rules needed adjustments to meet the changing temporal contexts. They were edited rather often: in the reigns of Parakramabhu I, Nissanka Malla, Parakramabahu П, Kirti Sri Rajasinha, and Rajadhi Rajasinha, with the usual goal to overcome the decline of *sangha*.[12] The chronicles, like the *Mahavamsa*, *Rajavaliya*, *Pujavaliya*, and *Nikaya Sangrahaya*, are also full of data depicting *sangha* in a miserable position. These chronicles contain contradictory facts; they give a description of a flourishing country full of monasteries and monks in saffron robes, where the kings patronize *sangha* and defend *dhamma* and at the same time nearly every ruler finds the Buddhist religion in decline and takes enormous efforts to purify the *sangha* and to reestablish the practice of *upasampada*.[13]

The periods of decline mentioned in medieval sources are so often (approximately every fifty years or even less) and so easily overcome by the momentous actions of various monarchs that they can hardly be considered signs of serious decay and as serious manifestations of structural crises in the development of Buddhism, a peril to its existence, impossible to neutralize. The image of the patron of *sangha*, zealous for its glory, added to the piety of the king, and purification of *sangha* from the *"dussila bhikkhu"* was, seemingly, a normal routine rather than an outstanding act.[14]

Medieval sources in Sri Lanka, aimed at the glorification of Sinhalese rulers through depictions of the deeds done to revive *sangha*, created a traditional historiographical scheme of the development of Buddhism on the island through the cycle of revival - decline - revival - decline.... This scheme is adopted by the majority of historians. The difference is in the usage of a particular term ("decline" can be replaced by decadence, decay, degeneracy, disorganization, fall, regress, collapse, etc.; "revival" by resurgence, renaissance, rise, succession, etc.) and in the determination of the chronological frames for the changing cycles.

The idea cultivated in the chronicles was reinforced in the works of European Christian missionaries, travellers, and colonial statesmen. They interpreted the religious syncretism of Sinhalese Buddhists and their tolerant attitude towards other religions not as an inevitable consequence of the history of Buddhism in Lanka (which incorporated all the pre-Buddhist beliefs and practices: Mahayana, Hinduism, and various trends of Theravada itself), but as indifference, ignorance, and a reflection of the state of decline of Buddhism on the island.

Ethnic and religious pluralism in the society in Sri Lanka—a kind of interdependent, intertwined, pluralism within the conditions of the day-to-day mixture of its various groups—created a peculiar cocktail of religious beliefs in Buddhist Theravada society. Transformations of the religious culture of Sri Lanka can be viewed along the lines of accommodating and assimilating newly-imported ideas. The syncretism of these Buddhist beliefs is a signal characteristic of Sinhalese Theravada on every level of religious consciousness, and the inclusive character of Buddhism here answers more for the longevity and survival of the discipline than for the degradation of tradition.

The development of *sangha* should rather be interpreted through the coexistence of two tendencies (and not through the categories of the "decline-revival" schema):

a. Sangha is tolerant to mass religion and incorporates popular practices;
b. Sangha neglects village religions and adopts the ideal of "pristine purity."

Actually, there was no strict barrier between a number of *sanghas*: the *transcendental-pragmatic* (H.-D. Evers,[15] E. Leach[16]), the *ascetic-village* (E.M. Mendelson[17]), the *canonical-traditionalist* (H. Bechert[18]), the *elite/intellectual-popular/mass* (E.R. Saratchandra[19]), the *Great Tradition/Little Tradition* (G. Obeyesekera[20]), and the *Buddhism of Nibbana/Buddhism of Dhamma* (J. Halverson[21]), but a great variety of complex, combined forms and interpretations of Buddhism.

Sangha was always an organism spontaneously reacting to developments in the socio-cultural, political, and economic spheres, demonstrating the highest adaptive capabilities for existence both in the centralized state and in the situation of distributed polity. *Sangha* didn't create a central organization controlling the whole system of religious institutions on the island; it existed as a combination of dispersed local monastic institutions maintaining a certain mode of life.

Differentiation of *sangha* is expressed in the chronicles in various ways: it is divided into *nikayas, ganas, mulas, ayatanas, viharas,* and *pirivenas,* each term bearing its shade of meaning. The term "*nikaya*" does not have a negative connotation, being neutrally a part of the whole (as *Tipitaka* consists of its parts, *nikayas,* which are not contradictory, but interactive).

The process of fragmentation, then, can be viewed not as a regrettable lack of unity (the striving for unification meant the search for a doctrinal identity, rather than an organizational one), but a way of vital activity, a general law of the existence of Buddhist religion: the traditional trend provides continuity within its development, while the reformist trend makes it appropriate to modern life.[22]

The periods of political decentralization had their own positive side. Despite the localization of the scale of activities, each separate *nikaya* received independence for organizational and doctrinal self-identification. The formation of schools, branches, and movements inside Theravada Buddhism led to the appearance of new chronicle traditions and commentary literature, and also strengthened the polemical potential inside monastic fraternities. Disputes were, in fact, regularly held. Besides, each monastery had a mechanism within itself for maintaining the balance between "purified Buddhism" and the popular religion, caused by the division of monks into three categories: *vanavasi,* on one hand; and *gamavasi* and *nagaravasi,* on the other.[23]

It is interesting to mention, that the term "decline"

doesn't work in conjunction with "dispersed *sangha,*" as well as "revival" with "unified *sangha.*" For example, the Revival of Buddhism in the late 18th and early 19th centuries brought to life a large-scale process of *bhikkhu* differentiation, and is usually proved in the literature by the rise of new fraternities both in Kandy (*Siam-nikaya* and its branches) and in the low country (*Amarapura-nikaya, Ramannya-nikaya* and their subdivisions).

Ceylon occupied an important strategic position in the Indian Ocean being situated on the commercial crossroads as a link between the traders of Middle Eastern and Far Eastern regions and possessing rich natural resources. The island became a colony at the beginning of the 16th century, first being invaded by the Portuguese (1505-1658), then by the Dutch (1658-1796) and then remaining a British crown colony during the long period from 1796 to 1948. European Christian powers neglected Buddhism as a state religion and *sangha* was deprived of state patronage. The Colebrooke-Cameron reforms of thirties-forties of the 19th century changed the political facade of the British crown colony Ceylon. The Legislative and the Executive Councils were established, and the representatives of the Ceylonese elite got the accession to the power structures. But the constitutional bias was weak and amorphous and developed under the initiative of British colonial administrators predominantly in the coastal areas of the South-Western province. This trend included liberally oriented British plantation-owners, burghers and converted to Christianity representatives of Sinhalese and Tamil elite strata.

The nationalistic middle-class groups of Ceylonese society took part in Buddhist revivalist movements under the slogans of religious character. They developed on the basis of traditional medieval reform movements within the *sangha* and evolved through the wide cultural and educational resurgence activities accompanying the political struggle for independence. These processes are traditionally depicted through the activities of the outstanding figures in the Buddhist world of the nineteenth century—Shri Siddhartha Thero, Hikkaduve Shri Sumangala Thero, Batuvantudave Devarakshita, Dharmakirti Shri Dharmarama Thero, Gunananda Thero, Anagarika Dharmapala.[24]

The stress is made usually on the strengthening of the reform tendencies caused by the British impact, on the affirmation of Sinhala-Buddhist identity and Buddhist nationalism in the anticolonial struggle. All this is viewed as a mainstream in the development of Buddhism in Sri Lanka, and even when there is a discussion among the scholars on the correlation of modernistic and traditionalist ideas in Resurgence movement, there is a tendency to seek for them within this trend, which is supposed to be the only one.[25]

But it should be admitted, that though we can trace the transformation of Buddhism through the colonial period, the most remarkable phenomenon was the way the Buddhist civilization preserved itself in spite of the impact of the established system, in which the link between *sangha* and state was broken. Though very important, Buddhist movements of socio-political protest possessing an anti-colonial bias were only a part in the development of Buddhist religious complex in the 18th and 19th centuries: traditional *sangha* continued its existence according to the rules, adopted ages before.[26]

The extent of movement activity is not necessarily equal to the extent of their influence in the society. The reformers had to win their place in the society, to prove their right to existence; their voice had to be loud to attract the attention of the Buddhist community, but they formed, by all evidence, a small part of the society. Buddhist reform movements were popular among the certain strata of urban population of coastal regions.

The developments inside Buddhist *sangha* in the colonial period should be viewed as a continuation of its evolution in previous ages, and, actually, there is no gap. The argument concerning when the Buddhist Resurgence movement[27] started—on the verge of 18th and 19th centuries, in the 1830s, in the middle of the 19th century, or in the last quarter of the 19th century—seems to be artificial, because reform tendencies are an inherent feature of Buddhism and there were and still remain the deep permanent roots for it, while the colonial rule, though longtime, was a temporary one.[28]

Buddhist reform movements played a significant role in the formation of the national liberation struggle, but it had also an opposite side: it lead to the development of party system conscious of the ethnic and communal barriers. Radically oriented anti-colonial programs became firmly connected with religious ferment while liberal programs were based on secularism and opposed communal concept of the formation of legislature and party system. Religious motivations of Buddhist revivalist movements had its logical continuation in the growing confrontation between Sinhalese-Buddhists, Tamils-Hindu and Moors-Muslims and the creation of separate political parties inside these ethno-confessional groups.

The maintenance of the communal representation in the Legislative Council influenced the process of party formation on identical principles: the majority of the emerging political associations were based on ethnic and confessional dimensions.[29] The first political organization which united Sinhalese, Tamils, and Moors appeared only in 1919: it had much in common with Indian National Congress (INC) which existed in India since 1885 and even bore an identical name, the Ceylonese National Congress (CNC), but the political future of this organization was quite different from its Indian counterpart. Already in 1921 it went to a split and never was destined to become a national leader: Tamil representatives of this party formed a separate political association called Tamil Mahajana Sabha. Even the abandonment of the communal principle of the formation of the Legislative Council didn't bring any change into the party system existing. Along with the Ceylonese National Congress, representing the interests of the Sinhalese community, there were formed All-Ceylonese Tamil Congress, Ceylonese Indian Congress, representing the interests of the so called Ceylonese Tamils and Indian Tamils accordingly, and Ceylonese Muslim League, representing the interests of Ceylonese Moors.[30]

At the same time, Buddhism inspired a wave of cultural revival. Independence brought into political life the so-called "second wave of Buddhist revivalism" with its claim to declare Sri Lanka a Buddhist state. From early fifties Ceylonese society produced a political system based on the periodic changes in power of two main parties: the United National Party (UNP) and the Freedom Party (SLFP), which was formed in 1952 as a result of a split inside the UNP. The system of stabilized two parties alternative became a main feature of the political climate in Sri Lanka. The "Buddhist strategy" of Solomon Bandaranaike, continued then by Sirimavo Bandaranaike, was followed by UNP leaders as well.[31]

The problem of correlation between state and religion was always under focus in independent Sri Lanka: both nationalistic parties rule a country in turn under the constitution declaring Sri Lanka a Buddhist state. The Independence Constitution of 1946-48 forbade all legislation which discriminated on grounds of religion. This clause was not incorporated in the Constitution of 1972,[32] which declared Sri Lanka a Buddhist Republic. In the Constitution of 1978[33] the special position given to Buddhism was further strengthened. It coincided with the growing participation of the Buddhist *sangha* in the activities of the political parties of modern type and the formation of political parties of the socially active *bhikkhus*, for example, The United Front of *Bhikkhus* (Eksat *Bhikkhu* Peramuna).[34] The political activities of Buddhist monks increase the peculiarity of Sri Lanka political party system and influence the character of the relations between Tamil and Sinhalese communities.

Politically motivated *bhikkhu*, although they constituted an important group of the Buddhist *sangha*, did not prevail in number over the traditional majority of monastic communities who were living according to the prescriptions of "Vinaya-pitaka."

The history of *Sangha* is a constant search for an optimal mode of organization: from the maximum of dispersion to the maximum of centralization through various stages and forms between these two poles; from the rigid dimensions of traditionalism to the flexibility of reformism through complex, syncretic intermediate ideological systems, such as "Reform within Tradition" and "Tradition within Reform."[35]

Notes

1. *Culavamsa. Being the More Recent Part of the Mahavamsa* (edited by W. Geiger). p. 1-2. Colombo, 1953; *The Dipavamsa. An Ancient Buddhist Historical Record.* (Original Pali text with a translation into English by H. Oldenberg), 1879; *The Mahavamsa or the Great Chronicle of Ceylon* (edited by W. Geiger), 1908 [reprint: Colombo, 1950, 1960]; *Nikaya-Sangrahaya* (edited by W.F. Gunawardhana), Colombo, 1908; *Pujavaliya* (edited by Saddhatissa Thera), Ceylon, Panadura Press, B.E. 2478; *The Rajavaliya, or a Historical Narrative of Sinhalese Kings from Vijaya to Vimala Dharma Suriya 11* (edited by G. Gunasekara), Colombo, 1900; *The Rajaratnakaraya* (edited by S. De Silva). Colombo, 1907; *The Saddharmaratnakaraya* (edited by K. Nanavimala). Panadura, 1931; *The Saddharmaratnavaliya* (edited by D.B. Jayatilake). Colombo, 1936; *Thupavamsa. The Legend of the Topes* (edited by B.C.E. Law). Calcutta, 1945.

2. The role of Buddhist historiographical tradition in the formation of modern ideological constructions is vividly depicted in: Kemper, S. *The Presense of the Past: Chronicles, Politics and Culture in Sinhala Life.* Ithaca, NY: Cornell UP, 1991.

3. The place of the concept "Lankadipa = Buddhadipa" in the formation of Sinhalese nationalism is discussed in: Perera, F. *The Early Buddhist Historiography of Ceylon.* Gottingen, 1979.

4. For details see: Gombrich, R.F., *Precept and Practice: Traditional Buddhism in Rural Highlands of Ceylon.* Oxford, 1971; Gombrich, R.F. *Theravada Buddhism: A Social History from Ancient Benares to Modern Colombo.* L.-N.-Y., 1988; Gombrich, R.F., and Obeyesekere G. *Buddhism Transformed: Religious Change in Sri Lanka.* Princeton, 1988.

5. See, for example: Bechert, H. "Theravada Buddhist

Sangha: Some General Observations on Historical and Political Factors in its Development." *Journal of Asian Studies* 29.4 (1970): 761-778; Bechert H. "Contradictions in Sinhalese Buddhism." *Contributions to Asian Studies* 4 (1973). Leiden: 7-17.

6. Malalgoda, K. "Buddhism in Post-Independence Sri Lanka." *Religion in South Asia: Religious Conversion and Revival Movements in South Asia in Medieval and Modern Times.* Ed. Oddie, G A. New Delhi: Manohar, 1977: 183-189; De Silva, K.M. *Religion, Nationalism and the State in Modern Sri Lanka.* Tampa: U of South Florida Department of Religious Studies, 1986: 10-11.

7. Malalgoda, Kitsiri. *Buddhism in Sinhalese Society: 1750-1900: A Study of Religious Revival and Change.* Berkeley: U of California P, 1976: 6-8.

8. Obeyesekere, G. "Religion and Polity in Theravada Buddhism: Continuity and Change in a Great Tradition." *Comparative Studies in Society and History* 21.4 (1979): 626-639.

9. Mendis, G C. *Ceylon Today and Yesterday: Main Currents of Ceylon History.* Colombo: Associated Newspapers of Ceylon, 1963: 97-98; Goonewardena K.W. Ceylon. – Historiography of the British Empire. Commonwealth. Trends, Interpretations and Resources. Durham, 1966, p. 444.

10. See, for example: Holt J.C. *Buddha in the Crown. Avalokitesvara in the Buddhist Traditions of Sri Lanka.* N.-Y., 1991, p. 15-36; Obeyesekere G. "Social Change and the Deities: The Rise of the Kataragama Cult in Modern Sri Lanka." *Man* 12 (1977): 377-396; Obeyesekere, Gananath. *The Cult of the Goddess Pattini.* Chicago: U of Chicago P, 1984.

11. Mirando, A H. *Buddhism in Sri Lanka in the 17th and 18th Centuries, with Special Reference to Sinhalese Literary Sources.* Dehiwala, Sri Lanka: Tisara Prakasakayo, 1985: 115-116.

12. Ratnapala, Nandasena, ed.. *The Katikavatas: Laws of the Buddhist Order of Ceylon from the 12th Century to the 18th Century*. München: Kitzinger, 1971: 48-49.

13. Evers H.-D. "The Buddhist *Sangha* in Ceylon and Thailand: A Comparative Study of Formal Organizations in Two Non-Industrial Societies." *Sociologus* 18.1 (1968): 30-35.

14. See, for example: *The Dipavamsa. An Ancient Buddhist Historical Record. (Original Pali text with the translation into English by H.Oldenberg)*. L., 1879: 142, 221, 222; *Nikaya-Sangrahaya* (edited by W.F. Gunawardhana). Colombo, 1908: 96; Law, Bimala C, ed. *The Legend of the Topes: Thupawamsa.* Calcutta, 1945: 97.

15. Evers, Hans-Dieter. *Monks, Priests and Peasants: A Study of Buddhism and Social Structure in Central Ceylon : With 27 Tables.* Leiden: Brill, 1972.

16. Leach E.R. "Buddhism in the Post-Colonial Political Order in Burma and Ceylon." *Daedalus* 52.1 (1973): 29-54.

17. Mendelson, Edward M. *Sangha and State in Burma: A Study of Monastic Sectarianism and Leadership.* Ithaca: Cornell UP, 1975.

18. Bechert H. "On the Popular Religion of the Sinhalese. Bechert, Heinz, ed. *Buddhism in Ceylon and Studies on Religious Syncretism in Buddhist Countries: Report on a Symposium in Göttingen.* Göttingen: Vandenhoeck & Ruprecht, 1987: 217-233.

19. Saratchandra E.R. "Traditional Values and the Modernization of a Buddhist Society: The Case of Ceylon." Bellah, Robert N. *Religion and Progress in Modern Asia.* NY: Free Press, 1965: 109-123.

20. Obeyesekere G. "The Great Tradition and the Little in the Perspective of Sinhalese Buddhism." *Journal of Asian Studies* 22.2 (1963): 139-154.

21. Halverson J. "Religion and Psychosocial Development in Sinhalese Buddhism." *Journal of Asian Studies*

37.2 (1978): 221-232.

22. Ilangasinha, H B. M. *Buddhism in Medieval Sri Lanka*. Delhi, India: Sri Satguru Publications, 1992: 56-66.

23. Smith, Bardwell L. *Tradition and Change in Theravada Buddhism: Essays on Ceylon and Thailand in the 19th and 20th Centuries*. Leiden: E.J. Brill, 1973: 36-38.

24. See, for example: Siriwardane C.D.S. "Buddhist Reorganization in Ceylon." *South Asian Politics and Religion*. Ed. Smith, Donald E. Princeton, N.J: Princeton UP, 1966: 531-546; Wickremeratne L.A. "Religion, Nationalism and Social Change in Ceylon, 1865-1885." *Journal of The Royal Asiatic Society (Ceylon Branch)* 2 (1969): 123-150.

25. Arasaratnam S. "Nationalism, Communalism and National Unity in Ceylon." *India and Ceylon: Unity and Diversity: A Symposium*. Ed. Mason, Philip. London: published for the Institute of Race Relations by Oxford U.P, 1967: 260-278; Arasaratnam S. "A Collective Look at the Transformation of Ceylon: 1800-1948." *Modern Ceylon Studies* 5.1 (1974): 107-110.

26. Mirando, A H. *Buddhism in Sri Lanka in the 17th and 18th Centuries, with Special Reference to Sinhalese Literary Sources*. Dehiwala, Sri Lanka: Tisara Prakasakayo, 1985: 115-116.

27. For the details in the discussion on "Buddhist Resurgence," see: Dharmadasa K.N.O. "A Nativistic Reaction to Colonialism: The Sinhala-Buddhist Revival in Sri Lanka." *Asian Studies* 12.1 (1974): 159-179; Reynolds, Frank E. "Tradition and Change in Theravada Buddhism: A Bibliographical Essay Focused on the Modern Period." *Tradition and Change in Theravada Buddhism: Essays on Ceylon and Thailand in the 19th and 20th Centuries*. Boston: Brill, 1973: 94-104; Farquhar, John N. *Modern Religious Movements in India*. New Delhi: Munshiram Manoharlal, 1977. Bond, George D. *The Buddhist*

Revival in Sri Lanka: Religious Tradition, Reinterpretation, and Response. Columbia, S.C: U of South Carolina P, 1988.

28. Bechert H. "Buddhism as a Factor of Political Modernization: the Case of Sri Lanka." *Religion and Development in Asian Societies.* Colombo: Friedrich-Naumann-Stiftung, 1973: 1-11; Evers H.-D. "Buddhism and British Colonial Policy in Ceylon: 1815-1875." *Asian Studies* 2.3 (1964): 323-333.

29. For details see: Kearney, Robert N. *Communalism and Language in the Politics of Ceylon.* Durham, N.C: Duke UP, 1967; Silva K. M. de. *Religion, Nationalism, and the State in Modern Sri Lanka.* Tampa, FL: Dept. of Religious Studies, U of South Florida, 1986.; Silva, K.M., de. *Managing Ethnic Tensions in Multi-Ethnic Societies: Sri Lanka, 1880-1985.* Lanham, MD: University Press of America, 1986.; Silva, K. M. de. *Ethnic Conflict in Buddhist Societies: Sri Lanka, Thailand, and Burma.* London: Pinter, 1988..

30. Silva, K.M. de, Shelton U. Kodikara, and K.W Goonewardena. *History of Ceylon: Vol. III. From the Beginning of the 19th Century to 1948.* Peradeniya, 1973: 350-352.

31. Silva C.R. de. "State Support in Contemporary Sri Lanka: Some Ideological and Policy Issues." *Sixth Sri Lanka Conference.* Peradeniya, 1997: 1-16; Bapat, P V. *2500 Years of Buddhism.* New Delhi: Publications Division, Ministry of Information and Broadcasting, Govt. of India, 1976: 388-414.

32. *The Constitution of the Democratic Socialist Republic of Sri Lanka.* Colombo, 1972: 5.

33. *The Constitution of the Democratic Socialist Republic of Sri Lanka.* Colombo, 1978: 8.

34. Silva K.M. de. *Religion, Nationalism, and the State in Modern Sri Lanka.* Tampa, FL: Dept. of Religious Studies, U of South Florida, 1986: 100-101; Huges J.J.

"Buddhist Monks and Politics in Sri Lanka." *Journal of Buddhist Ethics*. Spring Institute for Social Science Research, University of Chicago. April, 1987: 25-26; Katz N. "Buddhism and Politics in Sri Lanka and Other Theravada Nations since 1945." Fu, Charles W, and Gerhard E. Spiegler, eds. *Movements and Issues in World Religions: A Sourcebook and Analysis of Developments Since 1945*. Westport, Conn: Greenwood Press, 1987.

35. See: Roberts M. "Reformism, Nationalism and Protest in British Ceylon: The Roots and Ingredients of Leadership." Robb, Peter, and David Taylor, eds. *Rule, Protest, Identity: Aspects of Modern South Asia*. London: Curzon Press, 1978: 190-192.

Dr. Alexandra Safronova is a Professor Emeritus of the University of Moscow and Head of the History Department of the Institute of Asian and African Studies at Moscow State University.

CHAPTER 8

TATIANA SHAUMYAN

Netaji Subhas Chandra Bose: His Life and Fate

In 2006 the Institute of Oriental Studies held the Conference of Indologists of Russia and CIS countries. The need for the Conference could be explained mainly by the fact that after the collapse of the USSR scientific contacts between scholars in Indian Studies became very limited or even stopped. At the Conference we were able to gather the Indologists not only from Moscow and St. Petersburg, but also from Lipetsk, Irkutsk, Kislovodsk, and Penza, as well as our colleagues from Kazakhstan, Ukraine, Tajikistan and Uzbekistan. Later we published a collection of papers presented at the Conference.

The list of our colleagues prepared for the Conference included 123 scholars. Moscow was represented by 73 scholars; St. Petersburg, 15; 35 Indologists belonged to other cities of Russia and CIS countries. We wanted to obtain necessary information about the professional interests of our colleagues. The largest discipline represented was history (29 scholars). There were 24 linguists, 16 specialists in literature, 13 political scientists, 10 scholars of religious studies, 8 philosophers, 8 foreign policy experts, 7 economists, 5 ethnologists, and 3 art historians. I am afraid that an analysis of the list by age is unlikely to raise optimism; the majority of our colleagues are not adolescents.

Esteemed centers of scholarship like The Institute of Asian and African Studies of Moscow State University, Moscow State Institute of International Relations, Russian State University for Humanities, Department of World Politics of Moscow State University, and others, are all training specialists in Oriental Studies, but not so many of them wish to dedicate themselves to the study of South Asia. For us—the staff members of the Oriental Studies Institute and University professors—the question arises: what can we offer our young colleagues? Can they and their families survive on the salaries we offer them after graduation? We can't blame them for seeking a job in business or in those organizations that have nothing to do with their education, but can provide a comfortable existence. Therefore, our task is to look for opportunities to support the younger generation of professionals who are interested in working on India and the subcontinent. Without overcoming this problem, one can hardly expect a real continuity in the development of Indological Studies. And if we cannot engage a new generation in our studies, it is unlikely that we will be able to close the Open Pages in South Asian Studies. One of these pages is the life and death of the prominent figure of the liberation movement in India, a popular politician and public figure, quite contradictory and ambiguous, the great Bengali Subhas Chandra Bose.

The life and fate of the outstanding Indian politician is an open page not only for Russian Indologists; now nearly seven decades of scientists, military officers, diplomats, journalists and lawyers from India and the United Kingdom, Russia, Japan, and Taiwan are trying to reconstruct the events of the 1940s, and find multiple responses to their concerns about the fate of Subhas Chandra Bose. Was he was the victim of a plane crash over Taiwan, or did his life end in Stalin's camps? There are also other versions of his fate that are not more specific than the first two.

Many books and articles written by Indian, Russian, British authors has been devoted to the life, activities and the mysterious death of Subhas Chandra Bose. Therefore, there is hardly any need to go into the details of his biography, descriptions of the early period of his life and work. Our attention should be paid to the life of Subhas Chandra Bose on the eve of and during the Second World War, when the struggle of patriotic forces of India against the British colonial rule had intensified.

Subhas Chandra Bose went down in history as the hero of the Indians, a fighter for the liberation of India. Joining the Indian National Congress (INC), Bose made a brilliant career and became head of the party office in Bengal and a close ally of the Congress leaders Mahatma Gandhi and Jawaharlal Nehru. His supporters called Bose "Netaji," which means "leader."

British authorities arrested Bose for the first time in 1924—for taking part in the liberation movement—and he was sent to Burma to serve his sentence in prison in Mandalay. In 1927 Bose was released from prison and appeared on the political scene as the head of the young generation of the liberation movement in India. He called for the full national independence of India, a status above that of a Dominion, which was the position proposed by Mahatma Gandhi. After this, Bose was repeatedly arrested and put into British prisons. He used every opportunity to spread the ideas of the liberation movement and was continuously looking for allies in fighting against the British rulers.

In January 1938, at the Indian National Congress conference in Vishnupure, Bose outlined his program and action plan for revolution and independence based on the fact that India had matured. He stood for the Presidency of the INC, but his insistence on the use of force against the British caused an inevitable rift with Gandhi, and great dissatisfaction within the moderate wing of the INC.

In May of 1939 Netaji started an open fight against the Congress led by Gandhi, and after the formation of the Forward Bloc he began a propaganda offensive throughout the country. While the Forward Bloc was constituted as a political organization which would unify the left wing of Indian politics, its purpose was the uncompromising struggle against British imperialism. Bose sharply criticized Gandhi's idea of "non-resistance to evil," and his ambivalent foreign policy theories, which were also defended by Jawaharlal Nehru.

In September of 1939, after the beginning of the Second World War, Bose realized that world circumstances would allow India the opportunity to fight for its independence. On January 17, 1941 he secretly left his home in Bengal, illegally crossed the border of India, and reached Kabul, Afghanistan. There he negotiated with representatives of the governments of the USSR, Germany, and Italy for political asylum. Finally, on April 2, 1941, travelling under an Italian passport issued to the name of Orlando Mazotta, and a Soviet visa documenting his passing through Tashkent and

Moscow, Bose arrived in Berlin. After that date, his activities, in the opinion of many Indian patriots as well as British authorities and representatives of the anti-Hitler coalition, were extremely controversial.

Bose got an audience with Hitler, and he was allowed to form an Indian Legion of prisoners of war, 3000 in number, as well as to carry out anti-British propaganda on the radio and in newspaper publications. The Indian Legion was formed in April of 1943 as the 950th Infantry Regiment of the Wehrmacht. In November 1944 the unit was placed under the control of the SS, and its soldiers performed patrol and security services to strengthen the "Atlantic Wall" on the west coast of France. Bose's activity caused varied reactions both in India and in Britain. Being a patriot of his country and one of the most active freedom fighters, Bose believed that in the struggle for independence any means are both necessary and good. Apparently, he followed the well-known principle that "the enemy of my enemy is my friend." Therefore, in the struggle against the British colonialists, he was ready to take the help of Nazi Germany and militarist Japan. It was this position that created the image of Bose as a highly controversial figure: some considered him a true patriot and fighter for Indian independence, while others saw him as a traitor who collaborated with the most reactionary regimes.

In February 1943 Bose traveled first to Germany and then, after a visit to Tokyo, arrived in Singapore on July 2. There it became possible for him to rely on the more than two million Indians of Burma and Malaya. Compatriots welcomed him with joy, seeing him as their savior and leader.

Here, with the help of the Japanese, Bose formed a Government of Free India and the Indian National

Army, which consisted mostly of the Indian prisoners of war. As he created an Indian government in exile and declared war on Britain, Bose planned to have the INA invade India. On October 21, 1943 he offered the following statement on Singapore Radio:

> There is not the slightest doubt in our minds that when we cross the Indian frontier with our Army and hoist our National Flag on Indian soil, the real revolution will break out within the country — the revolution that will ultimately bring about the end of British rule in India.

One of the companions of Bose wrote that Indians joined the INA "with the sincere belief that they will come to India to fight for the freedom of their country."

In March of 1944, when the Japanese army started an offensive against the Indian city of Imphal, Bose decided that the time had come that he had long been waiting for: the INA now came to the territory of the homeland, and he was ready to send his entire army down to the last man. However, "the battle for India" and "march to Delhi," as such did not take place—Bose severely miscalculated. The initiative had been firmly in the hands of Britain, and the Japanese General Staff had planned an operation on a limited scale, designed to ensure the defense of Burma.

The attack on Imphal failed. Upon its entry into the territory of India, the INA did not meet with the response which was expected by Bose. The defeat at Imphal was a heavy blow to him. However, Bose would not acquiesce so easily, and he ordered the total mobilization of all human resources of the Free India movement. At the same time, he decided to change allies, and directed his attention then to the Soviet Union.

While in Japan in October of 1944 to speak to the students at the University of Tokyo, Bose attempted to contact the Soviet embassy there. He had hoped that his talk, which devoted a great deal of time to the influence in India of the October Revolution and the experience of socialist construction in the USSR, would open some doors for him with the embassy. He sent a letter to the Soviet ambassador in Tokyo, but the secretary of the Embassy returned the unopened letter to the courier.

Meanwhile, in February 1945, British troops began a decisive offensive in Burma, which ended with the defeat of the Japanese. The INA was in a hopeless position, and in May the main group surrendered in Rangoon. Twice, after the German surrender on May 8 and even after the beginning of the Soviet-Japanese war on August 9, Bose asked Tokyo to find an opportunity to discuss his trip to the Soviet Union. Although the Japanese government refused, the commander of the Japanese troops in Bangkok agreed to assist him.

Reports of Bose's last days are varied and conflicting. In one, Bose and his adjutant were given two seats on a Japanese bomber. The plane had to make a stopover in Mukden, where it was to leave Bose to contact the Soviet command. Before leaving he said to his interpreter: "I am ready to become a Russian prisoner. The only hope today is in Russia. I'm sure they still can face the British. And this will bring freedom to India. I am determined to entrust their fate to the Russians."

On August 17 a twin-engine bomber of the Japanese air force headed for Taipei (Taiwan), and landed safely. Pilots on the ground in Taipei discovered, upon inspecting the plane, a problem with the left engine, which they immediately repaired. However, when the plane took off from Taipei, eyewitnesses say that it reached an altitude of about 100 feet, then there was a loud explosion and the propeller and part of the engine fell out. The engine was destroyed, and the plane began to lose altitude rapidly. It hit the ground, broke into pieces, and burst into flames. Bose was badly burned and, along with other victims, were taken to a military hospital. On August 18, between 9:00 and 10:00 pm, Subhas Chandra Bose died of his burns. But a death certificate for Bose has never been found in the archives in Taipei.

According to the official version of the death, Bose's body was cremated on August 20, and the urn with his ashes was moved to the Buddhist Temple Tokyo at a Buddhist temple Renkōji in September of that year.

The last person to have seen Bose alive, Captain (Medical) Taneyoshi Yoshimi, gave a statement that resolved the matter:

> I personally cleaned his injuries with oil and dressed them. He was suffering from extensive burns over the whole of his body, though the most serious were those of his head, chest, and thighs. During the first four hours he was semi-conscious… he murmured, and muttered in his state of coma, but never regained consciousness. At about 23.00 he died. I injected Formalin into the body and also had the coffin partly filled with lime. The coffin was then taken away and cremated.

This version of the death of Subhas Chandra Bose in a plane crash in Taiwan has long been the subject of dispute. The Allied forces took the Japanese news as a ploy. The then-Viceroy of India, Field Marshal Archibald Wavell, noted in his journal: "I wonder if the

Japanese announcement on Subhash Chandra Bose's death in an air-crash is true. I suspect it very much; it is just what should be given out if he meant to go underground." As late as October 1946, the Government of India refused to confirm the death of Bose.

After the war, the name of Bose suddenly became very popular in India. There were rumors that the Japanese radio messages about the death of Bose were a bluff, and in reality Bose got to the Soviet Union, where he was gathering forces to fight for the liberation of his homeland. A little later, it was said that Bose was in the Soviet Union in prison, and died there. The British in every way sought to refute these rumors.

Nevertheless, in 1956 the Government of India appointed a special investigative commission headed by Shah Nawaz Khan, a former Lt. Colonel of the Second Indian National Army, with the participation of the elder brother of Subhash Chandra Bose, Suresh Chandra Bose. Two members of the commission came to the conclusion that Bose died in Taipei on the night of August 18, 1945, but Bose's brother did not agree with this view, and said that Bose was in the USSR. Therefore, the Indian parliament refused to formally approve the conclusions of the commission.

In 1970, the Government of India appointed a new commission of inquiry into the death of Bose. In order to avoid any dissenting opinions, this commission was actually a single person, G.D. Khosla, a retired chief justice of the Punjab High Court. His report was submitted in 1974, and he came to the same conclusion as the 1956 commission.

The secretary of the INA Defense Committee, Shyam Lal Jain, was deposed before Justice Khosla, and stated that on either 26 or 27 December, 1945, he had been summoned by Jawaharlal Nehru and asked to make typed copies of a hand-written letter with a vague signature at the bottom. Jain reconstructed the content of the letter from memory:

> Netaji reached Dairen in Manjuria at 1:30 pm on 23 August 1945, from Saigon by plane. The plane was a Japanese bomber. He had a plenty of gold with him in bars and ornaments. After disembarking, he ate banana and drank tea. He and four others, one of them a Japanese officer, Shidei, got into a jeep and went towards the Russian border. After about 3 hours, the jeep came back and gave the pilot instruction to fly back to Tokyo. (qtd. in Basu)

According to Jain, Nehru then asked him to type a letter to British Prime Minister Clements Attlee. In this letter Nehru wrote:

> I understand from most reliable source that Subhash Chandra Bose, your war criminal, has been allowed to enter Russian territory by Stalin. This is a clear treachery and betrayal of faith by the Russians as Russia has been an ally of the British-Americans, which she should not have done. (qtd. in Basu)

On 23 August, 1945, Sir Robert Francis Mudie, home member of the Viceroy's Executive Council, wrote a "Top Secret" note to Sir Evan Meredith Jenkins, Private Secretary to the Viceroy. It was for the consideration of the British Cabinet, and concerned the treatment of Bose. Mudie offers six options for the British, and states: "In many ways the easiest course would be to leave him where he is and not ask for his release. He might, of course, in certain circumstances, be welcomed by the Russians" (*Transfer of Power* 138-139).

In a memo dated 20 October 1945 and addressed to the India and Burma Committee of the British Cabinet, Bose is named a "dangerous suspect" for his alliance with the enemy in South East Asia. The India and Burma Committee of the Cabinet deliberated, with the Prime Minister present, concerning this situation on 25 October 1945, and concluded that Bose was a significant "civilian renegade." This decision clearly indicates that Bose was alive in October of 1945.

The Indian government continued to attempt to clear up this mystery with the help of Soviet leaders. In 1973, during the visit to Delhi of Leonid Brezhnev, a leader of the Socialist Party of India, Samar Guha personally handed to the Secretary General of the CPSU Central Committee a three-page memorandum outlining the reasons for doubt about the death of Bose, and requested that Soviet officials affirm or deny the story that Netaji had visited the USSR. Guha did not receive a response to his official inquiry. A similar request was made of Mikhail Gorbachev in 1988 by the head of the Socialist Party of India. Once again—a dull silence.

Stories like this continue for years. In 1992, a Forward Bloc party delegation met with Indian Prime Minister Narasimha Rao and demanded a new objective investigation into the disappearance of Netaji. Both the party and Janata Dal MP Samar Guha continued to work tirelessly on the mystery surrounding Bose's death and/or disappearance. In the same year, Guha requested that Russian President Boris Yeltsin inform the people of India about what is known to the Russians "of the fate of the great revolutionary hero fighting for the freedom of India." And again, this request was met with silence.

In 1999, following a court order, the Indian Government led by the BJP, formed another Commission of Inquiry, headed by a retired Justice of the Supreme Court of India, M.K. Mukherjee. The Commission was charged to address the following questions:

a. Whether Subhas Chandra Bose is dead or alive;
b. If he is dead, whether he died in the plane crash, as alleged;
c. Whether the ashes in the Japanese temple are the ashes of Netaji;
d. Whether he had died in any other manner, at any other place and, if so, when and how; and
e. If he is alive, where he is now residing.
("Air Crash")

The members of the Commission perused hundreds of files on Bose's death, collecting materials and documents in Japan, Russia, and Taiwan. In light of the evidence and arguments witnesses placed before the Commission, it arrived at the following conclusions:

a. Netaji Subhas Chandra Bose is dead;
b. He did not die in the plane crash, as alleged;
c. The ashes in the Japanese temple are not of Netaji;
d. In [the] absence of any clinching evidence a positive answer cannot be given; and
e. Answer already given in (a) above.
("Air Crash")

However that may be, members of this Commission didn't just disprove the air crash story; they opened the way for further inquiry, maintaining that Subhas Chandra Bose had disappeared while heading toward the Soviet Union.

I do not set out to pass a verdict on the real events related to the personality, life, and fate of Subhas Chandra Bose. My goal is to show that in the history of India since the end of World War II, there are a number of open pages which not only affect the interests of New Delhi, but require in-depth analysis of materials from Russian archives by Russian and Indian historians and political scientists.

A huge contribution to the study of the fate of Subhas Chandra Bose has been made by our colleague, Purobi Roy, Professor of the Jadavpur University, who has devoted years of her life working in the archives of many nations and meeting with Soviet and Russian scholars and journalists. Her work could shed light on the events connected with the fate of Bose. Roy was directly involved in the work of Mukherjee Commission, has repeatedly traveled to Moscow to work in a number of archives, and visited the Institute of Oriental Studies. In her affidavit filed with the Mukherjee Commission of Inquiry, she addressed "the particulars of the documents which might have come to her notice in course of her research and considered by her to be relevant for the purpose of the enquiry by this Commission."

Roy's summary of her analysis of multiple archival materials bears an extensive excerpt here:

> The general belief is that, after the formation of the Provisional Government of Free India, it was recognised by the countries belonging to the Axis Powers. But the records show that the USSR also recognised the Provisional Government. Besides, Mr. Pramod Mehra, of the National Archives of India, New Delhi, in March 1999, presented a seminar paper at the Netaji Institute of Asian Studies, Calcutta. In his paper on "The Declassified Documents from the Ministry of Defence"... he mentions "The recognition of the Pro-

> visional Government by the world powers, viz. Japan, Burma, Germany, Italy, Thailand, Philippines, [and] Russia declared the firm resolve of the Provisional Government to prosecute their struggle for India's freedom." (file No. 265, National Archives of India)
>
> Further, records which [have been] unravelled from the Russian and British archives clearly indicate that Subhas Chandra Bose was all along trying to go to the Soviet Union, and was seeking their help because he thought that the USSR [would be] the ideal place for arranging India's freedom struggle....The USSR also... maintained a positive attitude towards Netaji Subhas Chandra Bose and the Provisional Government of Free India.
>
> And finally, information obtained from reliable sources reveals that the classified documents on Netaji and the INA in the Russian archives confirm that Netaji Subhas Chandra Bose was in the Soviet Union up to October, 1946. (Affidavit)

What appears to be more interesting is the existence of unearthed materials hinting at Bose's contact with Soviet leaders, asking for arms help, later recognition of the Provisional Government of Azad Hind by the USSR, the activities of Soviet agents in India during and after the World War II, and other interesting information.

Meanwhile, in India the more and more prevalent belief is in "the Soviet version," that Bose ended his life in the USSR. As proof is given, for example, a secret British intelligence report, which states that in early 1946, Bose sent a confidential letter to Jawaharlal Nehru, notifying him that he, Bose, was imprisoned in the Soviet Union.

In 2006, Dr. Dipak Basu, a Professor in International Economics at Nagasaki University, wrote: "The statements by the INA officials, Japanese military officials, British intelligence reports, and The Top Secret Files published by the Brutish government in 1976 all say Netaji was alive in Soviet Russia." Basu continued:

> The British intelligence has reported that Nehru knew where Netaji was. Nehru took the Foreign Affairs portfolio himself and appointed none other than Vijayalekshmi Pandit as the ambassador to Russia. After her term was over, Dr. S. Radhakrishnan became the representative to Russia. Dr. Saroj Das of Calcutta University told his friend, Dr. R.C. Muzumdar, that Radhakrishnan had told him that Netaji was in Russia. Radhakrishnan couldn't come before the Khosla commission due to ill health and treatment in Madras. ("Mukherjee Commission")

I could quote more documents with evidence of Bose being in Russia. George Mukherjee, son of Abani Mukherji—one of the founders of the Communist Party of India—told him that his father and Netaji were prisoners in adjacent cells in Siberia. There is another version, according to which Bose returned safe and sound from the USSR in 1948 as an itinerant *sadhu.*

Thus there are several conflicting versions of the last years of life and the fate of Subhas Chandra Bose: from his death in a plane crash over Taiwan or in Stalin's prison, to his secret return to India in the guise of a holy man.

And if the point of view of Purobi and her colleagues from the Mukherjee Commission does not coincide with the conclusions made by many Russian and foreign scholars, it should be an additional stimulus for us to intensify our efforts to ascertain the real circumstances of the life and destiny of Subhas Chandra Bose. This will be a significant contribution to the elimination of Open Pages in Indological studies.

Works Cited

"Air Crash Did Not Take Place . . ." *All India Forward Bloc.* n.d. <www.forwardbloc.org/mukherjee_commission.html>.

Basu, Dipak. "Mukherjee Commission and the Mystery of Netaji's Disappearance." *Ivarta.com.* 3 June 2006. <www.ivarta.com/columns/OL_060603.htm>.

———. "Russia & Netaji." *New Delhi Statesman.* 2 February, 2011. <http://www.thestatesman.co.in/>.

Transfer of Power in India, 1942-47 - Vol. 6: The Post-War Phase: New Moves by the Labour Government, 1 Aug. 1945-22 Mar. 1946. London: Great Britain Foreign and Commonwealth Office, 1975.

"Mission Netaji writes to Honourable Chief Minister." 2 February, 2010. < http://www.missionnetaji.org/news/mn-writes-honourable-chief-minister>.

Noorani A.G. "Bose & the Nazis." Review of *Subhas Chandra Bose in Nazi Germany: Politics, Intelligence, and Propaganda, 1941-1943. Frontline* 29.12 (16-29 June, 2012). <www.flonnet.com/fl2912/stories/20120629291208100.htm>.

Roy, Purabi. "Affidavit." *The Enigma of Subhas Chandra Bose.* Hindustan Times. 1997. <www.hindustantimes.com/news/specials/netaji/purabi.htm>.

———. "New Findings on Netaji Subhas Chandra Bose: Russian, British, and Indian Archives." Unpublished manuscript.

Skosyrev, Vladimir. "Plane Crash or Hoax?" *Nezavisimaya Gazeta.* 19 July, 2005. <www.ng.ru/ideas/2005-07-19/11_crash.html>.

Vinayras. "Mukherji Commission & After." *Mission Netaji.* 20 June, 2008. <www.missionnetaji.org/article/mukherjee-commission-after>.

Dr. Tatiana Shaumyan is a Professor and Head of the Center for Indian Studies in the Institute of Oriental Studies of the Russian Academy of Sciences, Moscow.

CHAPTER 9

DOMINIK WUJASTYK

How to Choose a Good Indological Problem

I should like to begin by saying what a privilege it is for me to stand here today as a guest of the Russian State University for the Humanities and to be invited to offer some general reflections on a key process in academic life at this inaugural conference of this new centre for South Asian Studies. My sincere thanks to Professor Stolyarov and to all of your colleagues and to the university itself, for the kind invitation to come here.

A beginning is always a sensitive time, a time of balance, when even small words can continue to echo for many years. So I wanted to think carefully about what I might say today about choosing a good problem for research, especially in the field of Indology. I decided to try to say something a little more general, a little more reflective, perhaps, rather than dive into detailed Sanskrit or indological matters; to try to step back, and to think generally about this problem. All I can do is share some of my resulting reflections with you on this question of choosing an indological problem.

One of the battles that I think we all have to fight, and especially at the start of a new Centre for South Asian Studies, is the battle with the metaphors we use. We all live, and work, and think within a world of metaphors as was so elegantly shown by Lakoff and Johnson years ago in their book *Metaphors We Live By*.[1] We all of us, I think, in the academic field these days, feel pressure, feel that there is something difficult. Not just difficulties of Sanskrit interpretation or difficulties of epigraphy and so on, but that there is something difficult in our professional lives that we are struggling with. And very often that is a struggle for financial funding. We also struggle often for recognition, for positions at univeristies and so forth. And there is a strong sense of struggle in our field. I put this down firmly to the fact that our academic lives are lived mostly under the domination of inappropriate metaphors. That is to say, we are living in a world dominated by metaphors of business, of productivity, of customers, of finance. And that is, at root, not what we indologists do. We are not manufacturing a product in the same way that a factory produces a packet of fish. That is not what we do. We are generating new insights, moments of cognitive awakening, new knowledge. And if we are lucky we are creating a sense of revelation in our students. We may produce that moment when the student goes, "Ah! Yes! I understood something for the first time! Wow, that's interesting!" These are among the moments that define our professional lives. But we do not talk about them very much. And we do not talk enough to the people who pay us about how important the inappropriate governing metaphors are in distorting our professional lives.

I tried an experiment for a while, when I was working at the University of London. In the committee meetings that I went to, I quietly but systematically replaced the word "productivity" with the word "creativity." Thus, whenever one of our administrators or funding bosses would say, "Well, we have to think about productivity," I would say, "Yes, I agree, I think creativity is very important." Or, "When you say 'productivity' maybe we could also think about creativity?" I persisted with this. I was surprised by how well it was accepted. It was not received as something annoying; it was received as a change of view, with mild approval. I do genuinely believe two things: that the heart of what we do is creative work, not productive work, in any crudely economic sense, and that changing the language we use can lead to changes in thought and institutional policy. I feel that we should frame what we do, and the problems we choose, in Indology and in the wider field of South Asian Studies, from the point of view of creativity. And that has some ramifications for the metaphors that govern this meeting, the images of "open doors" and "filling lacunae," and finding out what it is that we do not know. I think it is important and admirable that Professor Stolyarov has framed this meeting. It does not happen often enough that a new initiative starts with such a beautifully open-ended opportunity for the examination the fundamentals of what we do. However, I also feel that the metaphor of, say, "blank pages," suggests that there is a book. And the book is nearly complete. But we need to fill it in a little bit, just finish it off, or put something there that is missing. All this rather contrasts with my idea of creativity. Rather than completing unfinished work, I see the activities that we engage in as scholars of South Asia as much more analogous to those of novelists or painters. We are creative people. We have an idea, and we follow it through. Something we write today did not exist before. We write our book, we write our article, and then it exists. It is a new object that is created out of our minds, and out of our personal interests and passions and enthusiasms. Of course it is controlled by the money we can raise, the people we talk to, and what is possible in our department, by what is available in our library, and all the other constraints. But, essentially, the core of it is a creative act, rather than the act of filling in a blank.

Thus, I think one of the first answers I would give to the question of how to choose a good indological problem is to say, well, let your enthusiasm and creativity run wild, and listen to your inner voice about this. I was pleased to discover, quite by accident, that somebody else has said all this already, in the context of molecular biology.

Figure 1 — Mendeley Bibliographic Database

This is how I made the discovery. I am quite interested in bibliography and the management of bibliographies. I think in five or ten years' time, the way we handle our bibliographies will be completely different. We'll all be just reaching into online databases, and the whole problem of formatting academic notes for a particular journal will probably fade away as an issue. It already is like this for many people in the sciences. One of the online bibliographical services that moves in this direction is called Mendeley. Some of you may have come across it. It is an interesting tool for managing your bibliographies on the hard drive of your computer, but also interacting with the web, and sharing information with other people. So you can set up a departmental bibliography, and so on. And there are other tools that do this, Citeulike, Zotero, and others. It is a growing world of activity. Mendeley is just one of them.

But Mendeley has some nice features. One of the things it does is publish tables of who is reading what. Because the Mendeley people have all this data provided by us, their users, they can very easily measure what we are all looking at. Here is one of the Mendeley pages, showing the most read articles in all the disciplines (see Figure 1). The numbers of readers given are not vast, because Mendeley is a fairly young service. But "How to Choose a Good Scientific Problem" as you see here, is number one on the science side.[2] Almost 2000 people have read that article. It is the top article on Mendeley, and it has been for months and months. It is just staying in that top position. I recognize that this is not the *New York Times* bestseller list, but it does give some measure of popularity for learned articles.

Uri Alon wrote the article, "How to Choose a Good Scientific Problem," and for most of a year it has maintained its place as the article that scientists most want to read. The numbers are telling in other respects too. In the sciences, people are reading things in the thousands, in the humanities it is ten, twenty, thirty, forty people. This mismatch is probably an artefact of the fact that Mendeley is presenting itself as a service for scientists more than the humanities. That is generally true for all online services, of course: these services are predominantly science-driven. It is also interesting to see—although the numbers are probably too small to be statistically significant—what people want to read in the humanities, namely "Imagined Communities" and so forth, and the classic article and book, "The Invention of Tradition." But it is also interesting to see the dates. Alon's article was published in 2009, and the second most popular science article was published in 2007, whereas the top two humanities articles are from 1991 and 1983 (for the famous Hobsbawm piece). It looks, from these (admittedly weak) statistics, as if people in the humanities are being much more strongly influenced by articles written 20 or 30 years ago than the scientists. The scientists are being influenced by what was written two or three years ago. Very different patterns emerge about how people, and how their disciplines, work. But, as I said, the numbers are too small to say anything statistically significant especially about the materials on the humanities side of the equation.

Having examined these trends, I thought I would join with the large number of other scientists and read what Uri Alon had written. It is a fine article, and is very interesting. On top of that, it is just two and one-half pages long, which is certainly refreshing! This is the wonder of it, that we all have time to read it. Alon says some surprisingly high-minded things in shuch a small space. I expected something grittier from a molecular biologist. But, for example, he says,

> Choosing a problem is an act of nurturing. What is the goal of starting a laboratory? [What is the goal of starting a Centre for South Asian Studies?] It is sometimes easy to pick up a default value, common in the current culture, such as, "The goal of my [Centre] is to publish the maximum number of papers of the highest quality." However, in this essay, we will frame the goal differently: "A [Centre] is a nurturing environment that aims to maximize the potential of students as scientists and as human beings."

He goes on to describe how choices such as these are crucial because values, even if they are not consciously stated, flow into all of the decisions, big and small, that are made in a Centre: what the Centre looks like, when the students can take a vacation, and what problems to choose. Alon then discusses how he feels the scientists in Molecular Biology should go about choosing a problem (see his graph here in Figure 2).

Alon gives two axes; one is "how much knowledge are we going to gain" and the other is "whether the research is hard or easy." In effect, he is saying: "Here is a group of problems that are very difficult, and we are not going to learn very much. Here are problems that are also very difficult, but they are potentially very rewarding, we are going to learn a lot. Here are problems that are very easy, but we are not going to learn a great deal. And here is a problem, just one, that is very faint, that is easy and it is a big-ticket question; we are going to learn a lot by doing that." One can imagine that a lot of our academic predecessors in nineteenth-century

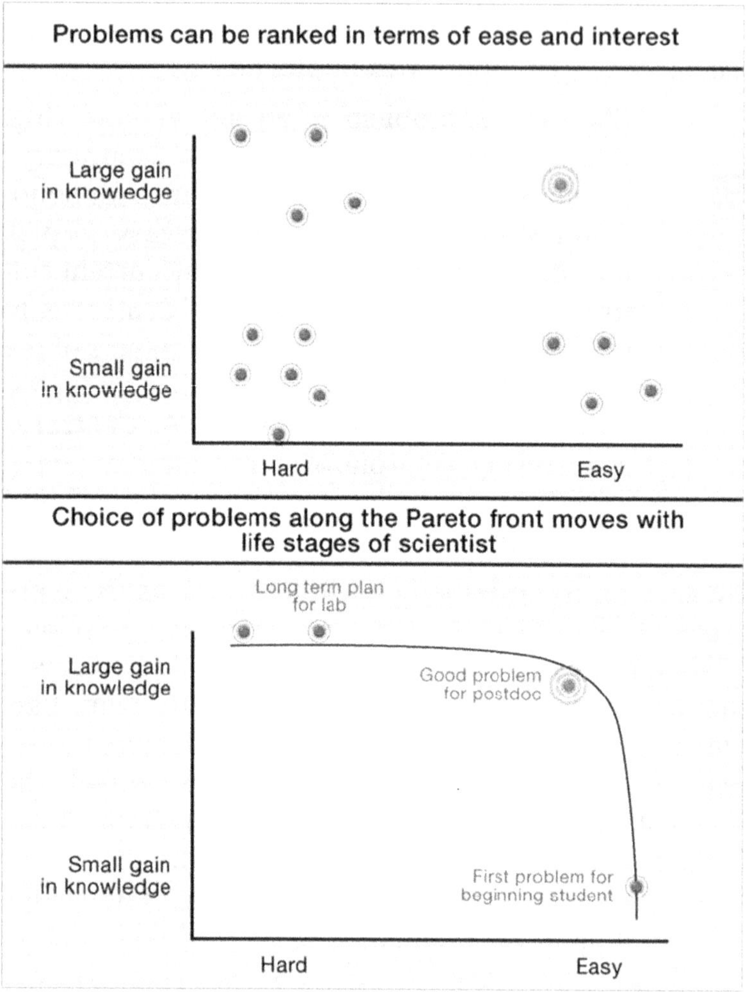

Figure 2 — Alon 2003, fig. 1

Asian Studies were picking off problems up there in the top right-hand corner, because the whole field was wide open and there was a great deal of new material. Almost anything one picked up told one a lot. We are not quite in that easy situation any more.

Alon then presents something that I do not fully understand, called a Pareto Front. I do not know if any of you have done enough economics to know what Pareto Normalization is; I have not. But it appears to be a statistical technique that allows Alon to draw a curve and to think a little bit more about where in a person's career these different kinds of problem may be addressed. So, the bottom right-hand corner—things that are easy and do not tell you very much—may be more suitable for students beginning in their careers. But problems where there is potentially a large gain of knowledge but great difficulty may be more suitable for senior scholars who have more experience and a lot of research already accomplished. But there is an even more valuable part to this paper.

Alon goes on to talk about nurturing students and guiding them to the choice of problems. One of the key points that he makes is that it is important to take time. He suggests that with students thinking about PhD topics, for example, at least three months thinking time is necessary. He recognizes that the problem that funding is difficult and that it is very hard to find three months and to last that long without having made a final choice about what you are going to do. But he emphasizes that before you commit to an academic problem, you should take at least three months to think about it yourself, to talk about it with your colleagues, to shake it around with everybody you can, and see whether it lasts with you as something you want to do.

The next point that Alon raises is that problems should be personal; we must have a personal enthusiasm for the project. We should listen our inner voice. Alon says that there are two voices that we are likely to hear. One is a loud voice of the interests of those around us, in conferences, in our department, and so on. The other is the faint voice in our breast that says, "this is interesting to me." Alon says that if you rank your problems with regard to your inner voice, you are more likely to choose problems that will satisfy you in the long term. He then talks about strengthening this inner voice, and about how the mentors, the professors or supervisors in a department, can help students to listen to their inner voice. One of the ways he suggests of strengthening this voice is to ask, "If I were the only person on earth, which of these problems would I work on?" Or, "How does it feel to describe your research to another person?" And he offers some other keys to thinking about what you personally are interested in. He talks about reflecting upon your own world view, again with the help of your mentor.

I was lucky enough in my own career, when I was just beginning doctoral research, to meet a pandit from Benares who said to me, in slightly different words, "have you got fire in your belly, are you excited about this, do you really, really want to do this?" I said, "yes, I really do!" And he said, "Good, because it is a long process, and you will get tired and frustrated, and only if you are personally committed, personally enthusiastic will you have the energy to last through those difficult periods, and do this piece of academic work that may last three, four, or five years." This is exactly Alon's point. Alon then talks about writing, deprecating the linear view—"I am starting here and finishing there"—when compared to a model of academic writing that is more open and has fluid pathways.

I recommend Alon's paper as a short, refreshing piece that refocuses attention on the highest goals of academic work and the inner dispositions that determine the success of our working lives.

I have emphasized creativity and listening to your inner voice, and making your choices about the problems you want to work on that are anchored in your own personality, that are personal choices. This approach leads to more interesting research and strengthens the researcher's ability to persist with a project for long periods. In our field of Indology, some of the most interesting recent projects that we have seen come precisely out of this kind of personal interest. I am thinking of James McHugh's PhD at Harvard a little while ago on scent and smell in Ancient India.[3] It is a new idea: that would be obvious. It is not a subject that has much of a history of scholarship behind it. But McHugh has written a fascinating and important book on this topic. I think Sheldon Pollock's work on epigraphy is very interesting because of his different way of thinking about inscriptions.[4] For Pollock they are not purely historical data, but a kind of literature, a kind of poetic expression (*kāvya*). Pollock also thinks about the uses of language by maharajas in the past and the relationship between language and political power in the early Sanskrit world. I think of the work of Joanna Jurewicz, that illustrates another point. Jurewicz's new book is on fire and cognition in the *Rigveda*.[5] I think that illustrates another point that is very important for all of us in thinking about academic problems and where to place our energies. Jurewicz has used a newly-developed field of linguistics, Cognitive Linguistics. This field was new to me; until I got her book, I didn't know much about it. But this new development in linguistics, a different way of thinking about metaphors and structures of texts and so forth, has allowed Jurewicz to revisit the *Rigveda*, one of the most-studied artefacts in our field, and come up with new information, new knowledge, new ways of looking at it, and a whole new argument about what the *Rigveda* is doing. Jurewicz now feels, and feels that she can prove, that the *Rigveda* is a far more coherent philosophical text than was thought in the past. She has also been able to discover new things about the *Rigveda*; for example she has argued that the doctrine of rebirth, *punarjanma*, is quite definitely present in the *Rigveda*. This is something that, as a student, I was taught to question, so a new argument on this point is welcome.

There are several other external academic fields that have a lot to offer us Indologists in the way of methodologies and ideas. Two examples are Intellectual History and Cultural History, neither of them particularly new, although the latter has been enjoying a resurgence recently.[6] Sheldon Pollock's project, "Sanskrit Knowledge Systems on the Eve of Colonialism" (SKSEC) ran from 2002 for several years.[7] As a direct result of this project, the words, "knowledge systems" etc., have started to be used rather freely in the field of Indology, especially in India. People unrelated to the SKSEC project now talk about "eve of colonialism" and "Sanskrit knowledge systems" as established categories of thought. The latter expression just means śāstra – there's no magic about it – but by using innovative language, it creates English discourse that enables people to relate to the concepts in an interesting and different way. The same is true of the phrase "intellectual history." Through the work of the Early Modern project, as one might call SKSEC, people are now talking about Sanskrit intellectual history in a way that did not happen before, and that in some cases brings the world Sanskrit intellectual endeavor into interesting comparison with pre-modern Europe. The focus on the early modern period, and using the phrase "early modern" to describe the period from 1550 to 1750, is a little controversial, and requires discussion. Historical periodizations always do. But people are settling into this, now that we have discussed what we think we mean, and there are enough publications about whether we will allow ourselves to use the phrase "early modern." Now we are talking quite happily about the early modern intellectual period in India. Nobody did that ten years ago. Formerly, this was not an umbrella under which you could publish an article or hold a conference, or do a book. But now it exists as a way of talking about the field.

I feel that the introduction of new language, terminology, and ways of looking at Classical Indian Studies that draws other adjacent fields of Humanities is very important. And this is perhaps the second major point I should like to make today. In order to survive as a field, we really need to integrate our studies into the global intellectual world. It is no longer really possible for somebody to sit in their study, have one student per annum, and do a critical edition of a 500-page manuscript. I know from personal experience that there are enormous intellectual pleasures to be had by working like that. But we are seeing centres for South Asian studies closing down one after another. In Britain, for example, the professorship in Sanskrit at Cambridge was lost, because Professor Brough did not prioritize student numbers. He was a great scholar, and has made huge academic contributions, but after he left, the professorship was cancelled and the department nearly folded. And a few years ago they announced that Sanskrit would no longer be studied at Cambridge. It may survive, but the situation is not certain. There is no longer a professorship of Sanskrit at London University since Professor Wright, nor at Edinburgh since Professor Brockington. An isolationist approach leads to the closure of our departments. We have to communicate. We have to convince our colleagues in classical studies, in anthropology, cultural studies, intellectual history, art history, that actually India is interesting.

And that means we have to adapt our language and modes of thought, and we have to communicate. We may lament the passing of an earlier style of scholarship, of a depth and detail of knowledge of Indology. But there are gains too, and we should focus on those.

When I was preparing the talk for today, I suddenly thought about Aurel Stein, who was an excellent example of this. Aurel Stein, as you know, undertook many expeditions, at the turn of the twentieth century, into Central Asia, and the Taklamakan Desert, and discovered a wealth of physical treasure in the form of manuscripts and paintings, but also a wealth of new knowledge about early Central Asia and indeed about early India.[8] After all his major expeditions Stein produced two publications. He published a scientific series of books: these were long, perhaps four volumes or more, huge scientific reports on what had happened, with catalogues of the artifacts that had been gathered. But he also wrote a second series of books, one each after each expedition. These were for the public, describing where he had been, about the camels, the desert, the struggles through sandstorms, the mountain pathways strewn with human bones. These were extremely popular books. People loved them and read them avidly. They were printed and reprinted and circulated widely. As a result, Stein became very well known to the general public of his day, and increased his ability to raise funding from the Royal Geographical Society for his later expeditions on the back of his public persona. That is a lesson for all of us: we do well to communicate with a wide public.

My time is nearly up, and I would like to mention just a few more areas of indological endeavor that I believe will grow in the future. One of them, I think, is natural language processing. We are beginning to see the birth of a corpus of Sanskrit literature. We haven't quite got a corpus of Hindi or other major languages yet, but the corpus of Sanskrit is beginning to appear in the Kyoto Text Archive, the GRETIL repository in Goettingen, in the Digital Corpus of Sanskrit, in the SARIT repository that I am building, in the Muktabodha Digital Library Project, and in other places. I think it is really in the last five years that indologists have begun to take it for granted that the *Ramayana*, the *Mahabharata*, the *Rigveda*, and other major texts are online. It is all still a bit chaotic. But this is coinciding with announcements by, for example, Google, of their N-gram program, where they are presenting huge English language corpora with simple tools to query these corpora of language. With Google N-gram, one can, for example, search for all occurrences of the words "love" and "truth" in the 19th century, and so forth, and see very interesting patterns emerging about the changing meaning of words, and their frequency. Even very simple searches can be revealing: if you search for the word "war" and you see it rising in the years before the outbreak of the World War I. Some of these things are very simple, but they can nevertheless give great insight. We are on the verge of being able to do some of this kind of statistical work on Indian language corpora. I believe that this is an area of work that will grow; I am not the only person who thinks this.

A few months before this conference, in a public discussion on computational linguistics, the question was asked, "is computational linguistics the new computer science for the humanities?"[10] There is a lot of material about this topic, and there are many informed people who think that this is going to be really important. It has been bubbling away under the surface for twenty or thirty years, but perhaps now is the time when this can become really important for a wider group of scholars. Because of the corpus of Sanskrit literature that is now available, this is going to be something that will affect our field.

There are many other subjects. The history of food, for example, I think is an area that is ripe for development. The history of emotions could be fascinating in our field. It is not very much studied anywhere; it is considered part of cultural studies in most universities in Europe and the USA. And I think that the study of the history of emotion could be very fruitful if applied to the South Asian case. I also think that we have a long way to go in re-theorizing caste. There are people here today with much greater expertise than I in this field. But I think that we are still working with ideas about caste that do not fit reality on the ground, and that are not sufficiently theorized. I feel that this is an extremely critical subject for modern India, critical for social and modern historic reasons.

As part of the same discussion, we in Indology need to theorize Sanskrit more deeply than we have in the past. We need to think explicitly about the attitudes surrounding the Sanskrit language, from the idea that this is the language of God, through the idea that it is a highly privileged language, to the ridicule that is sometimes heaped on Sanskrit as an absurdly theoretical topic of study.[11] In English, Sanskrit is often used as a word for something completely arcane and useless, most famously, perhaps, in Bernard Shaw's *Pygmalion*, when Professor Higgins says, "Do you know Colonel Pickering, the author of *Spoken Sanscrit*?" That is presented as a joke: here is a man who does something impressive but completely useless. Attitudes to Sanskrit, I think, need to be examined and theorized carefully.

I was very shocked, and perhaps one should not be, when I was recently re-reading Ronald Inden's book *Imagining India.*[12] It is a widely-read book that I, and perhaps many people, think is profoundly misguided. It can be read as a sustained and often misguided attack on Brahmans and on Sanskrit culture generally. We need to continue the professional discussion about what Sanskrit is, and what its complex basis in the social life of India has been.

Please allow me to conclude by summarizing just some of the key points that I would like to leave with you today. In order to survive and prosper, there are a number of things we must do:

- Systematically replace "productivity" with "creativity" in our thinking.
- Be prepared to surprise yourself and others in matters of scholarship.
- Ask bold, probing questions, and try to bring to the fore of your mind those niggling uncertainties that have always irritated you.
- Be aware of the forces at work, external to Indological scholarship, not only in popular fields such as yoga and ayurveda, but also the polarization caused by the fundamentalist thinking related to politics in contemporary India. That's a big discussion that we cannot really have today, but it deeply affects our field.
- Nurture the strengths and interests of the people already in the department. Identify their interests, support them, and nurture their talents. Give them the freedom to work, and encourage them to write by showing interest in what they do and providing support where necessary. Commensality is an extraordinarily powerful tool for enhancing academic communication, as has been understood in the

older universities since the twelfth century.

- Study the general trends of scholarship over recent decades in Europe and North America. Indologists always trail behind everybody else, because the field is small and under-funded. We should observe what the classicists, the historians, the anthropologists and the philosophers are doing elsewhere.
- Finally, and with perhaps a slightly depressing note at the close, study the availability of funding. Be prepared to work hard at fundraising, even dedicating staff specifically to this task. Consider hiring external experts in funding applications. Grant application procedures are commonly difficult and time-consuming, to say the least, but there are extremely large amounts of money at stake. In some cases there is funding for teams of people to work together for many years. But to get it is extremely hard, not intellectually but administratively. So we should think professionally and strategically: for example, there are specialists who will work on a no-win no-fee basis preparing European Research Council grant applications. This may sound a bit shocking; we scholars are not accustomed to thinking like this. But I believe that today we have to think like this. We have to think seriously about learning the language of funding applications. We should share our successful application documents with each other, and learn from each other. If you have made an application and got the funding, put your application on the internet, so that colleagues can see the language you used, and the scheme you laid out, and don't be too fussy about "talking the talk," that is, tailoring your language to get the money. Because if you just talk like an

> nineteenth-century indologist, you won't get your funding. You have to use phrases like "cultural flows across boundaries," whose meaning may be puzzling, but that succeed in attracting funding. And of course once you have the money, you can do the Indology.

Good luck with all these processes, and congratulations on the birth of this new Centre!

Notes

1. George Lakoff and Mark Johnson, *Metaphors We Live By* (Chicago, 1980).

2. Uri Alon, "How to Choose a Good Scientific Problem," *Molecular Cell* 35 (2009): 726-8.

3. Since published as *Sandalwood and Carrion: Smell in Premodern Indian Religion and Culture* (New York: OUP, 2013).

4. *The Language of the Gods in the World of Men: Sanskrit, Culture, and Power in Premodern India* (Berkeley: University of California Press, 2006).

5. *Fire and Cognition in the Ṛgveda* (Warsaw: Dom Wydawniczy ELIPSA, 2010).

6. Exemplified by the founding of the International Society for Cultural Studies in 2008 and the launch of its new journal, *Cultural History* in 2012.

7. <http://www.columbia.edu/itc/mealac/pollock/sks/>

8. Amongst several biographies, Jeannette Mirsky's *Sir Aurel Stein: Archaeological Explorer* (Chicago, 1977) is a good starting point.

9. Some collections are indexed at <http://indology.info/etexts/>.

10. <http://www.neh.gov/divisions/odh/grant-news/computational-linguistics-the-new-computer-sci-

ence-the-humanities>.

11. Sheldon Pollock's *The Language of the Gods in the World of Men* (Berkeley, 2009) is of course exactly such a study. The field bears expansion.

12. Bloomington, 1990.

Works Cited

Alon, U. "How to Choose a Good Scientific Problem." *Molecular Cell* 35.6 (2009): 726-728.

Inden, Ronald B. *Imagining India*. Bloomington: Indiana UP, 1990.

Jurewicz, Joanna. *Fire and Cognition in the R̥gveda*. Warszawa: Elipsa, 2010.

Lakoff, George, and Mark Johnson. *Metaphors We Live By*. Chicago: U of Chicago P, 1980.

McHugh, James. *Sandalwood and Carrion: Smell in Indian Religion and Culture*. Oxford: Oxford UP, 2012.

Mirsky, Jeannette. *Sir Aurel Stein, Archaeological Explorer*. Chicago: U of Chicago P, 1977.

Pollock, Sheldon I. *The Language of the Gods in the World of Men: Sanskrit, Culture, and Power in Premodern India*. Berkeley: U of California P, 2006.

"Sanskrit Knowledge Systems on the Eve of Colonialism." *The Sanskrit Knowledge-Systems Project*. Columbia University. 26 July, 2009. <www.columbia.edu/itc/mealac/pollock/sks/>.

Wujastyk, Dominik. "Virtual e-Text Archive of Indic Texts." *Indology: Resources for Indological Scholarship*. Indology Committee, BASAS. 2005. <indology.info/etexts/>.

Dr. Dominik Wujastyk is a Professor of Tibetan and Buddhist Studies, Department of South Asian Studies, University of Vienna.

CHAPTER 10

WILLIAM G. VANDERBOK

Where Are We Going? A South Asian Studies Trend Analysis

Modern area studies programs began in earnest the United States shortly after the Second World War. Prior to that time the US conceived of itself as a continental power protected by vast oceans and friendly neighbors. The popular mind still honored George Washington's admonition to avoid "entangling foreign alliances." The end of the war saw the collapse of our allies' colonial holdings and the emergence of the US as the only thriving industrial power with newly discovered global economic and security interests. A need to understand these far flung responsibilities assumed heightened importance. At the same time hundreds of thousands of soldiers were demobilized with full benefits awarded by the "GI Bill." Included in that package was the right to a federally subsidized college education. Universities underwent an enrollment explosion. For example, Harvard University went from 1,800 students in

1944 to 14,000 in 1947 to 21,000 today. Indiana University went from approximately 3,000 students to around 30,000 in just over a decade and currently enrolls over 40,000 on its Bloomington campus. The need for qualified faculty exploded at similar rates. The convergence of these needs supported the creation of area studies programs at the post-graduate level with Federal, state and foundation support on a scale hitherto unimaginable.

Federal dollars were directed at the most pressing foreign policy areas of the globe, initially Europe and East Asia. Later Latin America and Africa were added to the mix. Neither South nor West Asia figured significantly in the thinking of government policy makers interested in developing "bench strength," i.e., a substantial coterie of scholars familiar with the culture of the region, as insurance against future needs. India was left to a handful of Indologists and missionary groups interested in the Subcontinent. Significant funding was never made available, with a single caveat: Under the Eisenhower administration's PL480 legislation (renamed by President Kennedy "Food for Peace") the U.S. resolved a significant domestic political problem – over-abundant agricultural productivity in the politically important Midwestern states – by selling India surplus food grains for rupees and reinvesting those rupees in a variety of aid programs. In short order US government rupee holdings became so gigantic as to be a major source of friction with India. Eventually the PL480 debt was forgiven but not before several American universities were designated "national resource centers for India." [1] PL480 funds were used to provide them with massive amounts of published material from all over India. This publication purchasing program went on for forty years.

On the private foundation side of funding the premier source was the Ford Foundation, which opened its first international field office in New Delhi in 1952. Around the same time Ford announced a program of strengthening university area studies programs through a series of five year programs. East Asian, Latin American and African studies all benefitted. The year before it was South Asia's turn Ford underwent a leadership change and the program was cancelled.

This history somewhat explains why the US has an:

- African Studies Association
- American Oriental Society
- Association for Slavic, East European, and Eurasian Studies
- Association of Asian Studies
- German Studies Association
- Latin American Studies Association
- Middle East Studies Association
- Slavic Studies Association, but until very recently no...
- South Asian Studies Association.

State of the Area Study

Because there are over 4,400 degree granting institutions of higher education in the United States, it should come as no surprise that a limited number of them offered programs in Indian studies in the period immediately after the Second World War. With qualified professors in short supply, faculty senates provided generous grants supporting field research as an essential part of university recruitment efforts. Meanwhile, the Government of India (GOI) imposed increasingly stringent restrictions on the kinds of research it was willing to issue visas for. Need for coordination on the American side was called for. In 1961, under the leadership of W. Norman Brown, Professor of Sanskrit at the University of Pennsylvania, the American Institute for Indian Studies (AIIS) came into being as a non-governmental academic consortium to facilitate research on and in India. AIIS's primary focus traditionally has been on languages, art, archaeology and ethnomusicology. Initially supported by foundation funding, today it is primarily a re-granting agency (other agencies provide/grant the funds which it then redistributes). Its board membership consists of over 60 universities.

As part of its acknowledgement of modern India's 50th anniversary three past presidents of AIIS — Joseph W. Elder, Edward C. Dimock, Jr., and Ainslie T. Embree — were charged with chronicling the major advancements in our understanding of India over those five decades. The result was *India's Worlds and U.S. Scholars, 1947-1997,* published in 1998[2]. This makes *India's Worlds* a good starting point for examining the state of scholarship on South Asia. The book is organized by discipline and sometimes sub-discipline. There are chapters on:

- Anthropology
- Archaeology
- Art History (Islamic)
- Dance
- Economics
- Folklore
- Geography

- History (pre-colonial)
- History (colonial and post-colonial
- Languages
- Linguistics
- Literature
- Mathematics and Mathematical Astronomy
- Music
- Philosophy
- Political Science
- Religious Studies: Vedic and Classical Hinduism
- Religious Studies: Medieval Hinduism
- Religious Studies: Modern Hinduism and Jainism
- Religious Studies: Theories of Comparison
- Religious Studies: South Indian Hinduism/Buddhism/Jainism
- Religious Studies: Islam
- Sanskrit
- Theatre
- Women's Studies

These chapters, each prepared by a recognized expert in the field, cover 480 pages and average nearly 17 pages per topic. More succinctly, this breaks down as:

- Philosophy & Religion: 96 pages
- Performing Arts: dance, music, theater: 62 pages
- Sociology/Anthropology/Women's Studies: 76 pages
- Languages/Linguistics/Literature: 48 pages
- History: 42 pages
- Contemporary political and economic issues: 32 pages

The American Academy of Religion has a 400 member subsection devoted to South Asian religions so it is understandable that *India's Worlds* devotes significant attention to the topic. However, *India's Worlds* reviews nothing pertinent to the study of Sikhism or Zoroastrianism. Buddhism gets short shrift. There is nothing pertinent to Christianity even though St. Thomas the Apostle is buried in Chennai and Christian schools have educated a vast proportion of India's political, social, economic and cultural elites. Economics receives scant attention, a mere 12 pages, even though poverty and economic development have been at the heart of India's contemporary problems since Independence. Political science, broadly conceived, gets 20 pages with little to advance our understanding of Indian federalism, state politics, political elites, foreign policy or strategic policy issues. There is not even a significant literature comparing the widely divergent paths taken by the Indian and Pakistani military elites since Independence. To no small extent all of this is the direct result of the GOI's visa policy which for three decades was permissive of religious studies but very hostile to outsiders investigating contemporary issues with a political or policy component. It also attests to the fact that government funding of areas studies programs was exceedingly benign and largely devoid of current or midrange policy content.

Eight years later this stock taking was revisited in a special 143 page issue of the journal *India Review* entitled "The State of India Studies in the United States, 2006" edited by Sumit Ganguly and Alyssa Ayres.[3] Their introduction quite correctly argues that traditional American interest in Indian religion, art and philosophy stems from American Christian missionary involvement in the Subcontinent. Ignoring the withdrawal of Ford Foundation support, they note that the whole concept of area studies came under considerable academic criticism starting in mid-1980s in order to account for the failure of South Asian studies to take hold across the country. Instead of an in-depth understanding of individual countries and cultures the intellectual fashion shifted to a comparative understanding of many countries and cultures, and then something generally conceived to be more "scientific".[4] In my own discipline, political science, this took the form of formal theory, highly structured, statistical and mathematical modeling of political processes. In that now dominant view, traditional area studies are highly personal, judgmental, unscientific and, therefore, unreliable and intellectually unworthy. Also not mentioned by Ganguly and Ayres is the significant impact of Senator Frank Church. As chairman of the Senate Intelligence Committee, Church orchestrated a major redirection of intelligence resources from human intelligence to signals assets. In other words, government chose to place less reliance on people with country knowledge and more reliance on satellite and electronic surveillance. To universities this translated into reduced funding for language acquisition and area studies programs. Academic fashion, withered political funding, and sharply reduced foundation support coalesced to stunt area studies programs for over two decades.

Ganguly and Ayres argue that the 9/11 attack on the World Trade Center was a wake-up call driving new resources into area studies. This is an overstatement. A renewed interest in Islam and terrorism, perhaps, but African studies? Latin American studies? Asian studies? South Asian studies? Not in evidence.

Furthermore, significant new funding for South Asian studies has yet to materialize even though there is some movement to enlarge language training. Still, all Indian languages combined have an enrollment less than half that of Korean.[5]

What has happened to renew academic interest in South Asia as a focus of teaching and research is:

- India as a partner in restraining Chinese global ambitions (government perspective)
- India and Pakistan as a nuclear flash-point (government perspective)
- Growing financial and political power of the Indian diaspora in US politics
- Highest per capita income of any group in the U.S.
- Governors of two states
- Bobby Jindal in Louisiana
- Nikki Haley in South Carolina
- Attorney General of California (Kamala D. Harris)
- India as a rapidly growing economic power (business schools)
- Strong interest by second generation Indo-Americans in their ancestral heritage (arts & humanities perspective)
- Philanthropic interest by a few wealthy Indians (major gifts to Harvard, Cornell, UCLA, etc.)
- Some additional Federal government funds to support language training.

After their introductory essays, the Ganguly and Aryres review of South Asian studies offers chapters focusing on a variety of disciplines: economics, political science, religious studies, anthropology, and history. While similar to the chapters found in *India's Worlds,* the contribution by John Adams on economics stands out for its attempt to account for the minimal attention paid to India in American universities. Notable reasons mentioned are:[6]

- The idea of area studies conflicts with economists' desires to be universal in applicability. This is also true of political scientists.
- AIIS and other funding agencies demonstrate little interest in supporting economic research. This is also true of political science research.
- Working exclusively on India would carry negative weight in a tenure decision in an economics department. This is also true in political science.
- University officials prefer to use resources to strengthen disciplinary programs, not area studies.

Looking Toward the Next "State of the Area Study": Allocating Research Effort

South Asian studies is currently beset by low student interest, disciplinary trends hostile towards area studies and limited funding for field research. As such, scholars, particularly ones *without* tenure, must be careful where they place their research efforts. Professional conferences are a good indicator of where a field is trending, particularly since they are often the first place young scholars look to get themselves established.

To assess trends I looked at the programs of the three largest South Asian Studies associations, the European Association for South Asian Studies (EASAS, 2011), the South Asian Studies Association (SASA, 2007-2011), and the British Association for South Asian Studies (BASAS, 2008 and 2010), plus the university sponsored Wisconsin Conference on South Asia (2007 and 2011). Programs for all of these meetings are readily available on the Internet. I did not consider Association for Asian Studies conferences because their South Asia offerings are extremely limited. In reviewing the data that follow it is important to keep in mind that EASAS differs from the others in three important ways. First, EASAS is a biannual event, the others are all annual. Attendance is therefore higher in its service area because it is less frequent. Second, EASAS sets up topical sections which effectively solicit/encourage proposals in desired fields whereas the other three screen for appropriateness whatever is offered, unsolicited. Finally, EASAS restricts presentations to the colonial and post-colonial periods while the others accept papers regardless of historical period. The data source breaks down as (Table 1):

Table 1: Number of Papers by Conference

CONFERENCE	FREQUENCY	PERCENT
BASAS	140	8.8
SASA	372	23.4
EASAS	424	26.6
Wisconsin (WISC)	656	41.2
TOTAL	1592	100.0

Many argue that there is a great deal of cross-fertilization of ideas and research by scholars around the world. This may be true from a bibliographic perspective but does not hold when you think in term of networking and personal relationships. As shown below (Table 2), most participants in BASAS meetings are based in the UK (70%, 86% if West Europeans are added). Most going to Wisconsin live in the US (87%). Most attending EASAS are from Western Europe (56%, when UK residents are added in).[6] SASA draws 73% of its participants from the US. On the other hand, SASA does an outstanding job of drawing researchers from the Subcontinent in spite of the presumption that US visa procedures prevent participation from the region. In fact, 80% of all participants from Pakistan across all conferences attended a SASA meeting. SASA also does remarkably well drawing scholars from Eastern Europe, Russia and the smaller states of South Asia. Neither American conference draws interest from Western Europe nor does EASAS draw much American participation.

Table 2: Conference by Where the Presenter is Based

BASED IN	BASAS	SASA	EASAS	WISC	TOTAL
US/Canada	8	272	26	573	879
UK	98	24	28	37	187
W. Europe	22	6	55	11	94
E. Europe	1	5	1	0	7
India	3	21	29	12	65
Pakistan	0	20	2	3	25
Other S. Asia	5	10	3	5	23
Russia	0	2	1	1	4
Other	1	12	3	12	28
Unknown	2	0	276[7]	2	280
TOTAL	140	372	424	656	1592

I recall a conversation with a book seller at the Wisconsin conference more than two decades ago when I commented that there seemed to be more Indians in attendance that usual. His comment was that we were undergoing an "indigenizing" of the discipline as more and more US trained scholars decide to join the India diaspora rather than return home. That is certainly the case worldwide although more so for the US than for Europe (see Table 3).

Table 3: Ethnicity by Conference

SURNAME	BASAS	SASA	EASAS	WISC	TOTAL
European	73	153	241	314	781
Asian	66	219	182	342	809
Other	1	0	1	0	2
TOTAL	140	372	424	656	1592

Half of all US based presenters have South Asian surnames and 46% of those based in the UK but only 21% of those based in Western Europe (Table 4).

Table 4: Ethnicity by Base

BASED IN	ETHNICITY			TOTAL
	European	Asian	Other	
US	439	440	0	879
UK	99	87	1	187
W Europe	73	20	1	94
E Europe	6	1	0	7
India	5	60	0	65
Pakistan	0	25	0	25
Other S Asia	1	22	0	23
Russia	4	0	0	4
Other	9	19	0	28
Unknown	145	135	0	280
TOTAL	781	809	2	1592

As noted earlier, one of the major complaints with area studies is that they are not comparative but instead focus in on a single country or single region, however defined. In a nation as gigantic and diverse as India internal comparisons, not seen as comparisons at all by outsiders, can uncover enormous differences, often more dramatic than intra-European comparisons. Nevertheless, there is substance to the assertion that South Asian studies tend to be somewhat insular even though the same can be said of mainstream disciplines. SASA tends to be the most comparative conference, with nine percent of its papers comparing within or beyond the Subcontinent (see Table 5).

Table 5: Conference by Tendency to Compare

COMPARATIVE PRESENTATIONS	CONFERENCE				TOTAL
	BASAS	EASAS	SASA	WISC	
NO	127	410	338	646	1521
YES, IN REGION	3	7	13	4	27
YES, OUTSIDE REGION	10	7	21	6	44
TOTAL	140	424	372	656	1592

All of this is preliminary to where scholars are putting their research efforts and thus the areas where we can expect further understanding of South Asia and, by omission, defining areas where effort may be needed to develop additional research capability for the future (see Table 6).

Table 6: Conference by Discipline

DISCIPLINE	CONFERENCE				TOTAL
	BASAS	EASAS	SASA	WISC	
Strategic/ Military	3 2%	18 4%	26 7%	12 2%	59 4%
Political	29 21%	66 16%	68 18%	78 12%	241 15%
Economics	9 6%	23 5%	26 7%	16 2%	74 5%
Sociology	25 18%	134 32%	67 18%	94 14%	320 20%
Modern History	37 26%	35 8%	25 7%	63 10%	160 10%
Pre-Colonial History	5 4%	3 1%	18 5%	61 9%	87 5%
Hinduism	1 1%	19 4%	40 11%	29 4%	89 6%
Islam	1 1%	13 3%	7 2%	21 3%	42 3%
Other Religions	0 0%	0 0%	8 2%	24 4%	32 2%
Art/Music, etc.	11 8°/0	55 13%	70 19%	136 21%	272 17%

Political Science. When area studies first began after World War Two they were dominated by political scientists. Under the impact of funding cutbacks and shifting academic fashion, political science themed papers now account for only 19% of all presentations. Of that a scant 4% involve issues of strategic concern—Kashmir, the Afghanistan conflict, terrorism, Indo-Chinese relations, etc. Political presentations are likewise highly circumscribed with little or no attention being paid to public policy analysis, political party institutionalization or the impact of religious nationalism, to name just a few topics. On the other hand, considerable attention is being paid to subaltern and dalit politicization.

Economics. John Adams' comment in the already discussed special issue of *India Review* is cogent; economists do not work well with non-economists. Only five percent of the nearly 1,600 presentations can in any sense be considered economic and that is a stretch because papers entitled something like "Karnataka Dalits, Land Reform and Economic Justice" and "Women and Micro financing" were coded as economic rather than political or sociological in nature. Papers on trade relations, economic growth and development, foreign direct investment or even tax policy are virtually unheard of.

Sociology. Sociology is easily the most heavily represented discipline, comprising 20% of all presentations. At the European Association it is one-third of all presentations, although only 18% at BASAS and SASA and 14% at Wisconsin. The "miscellaneous" category at the bottom of Table 6, however, is about one-third women's studies presentations — a separate category in the India's Worlds review. Relocating those presentations to sociology would raise sociology to approximately one paper in four.

History. Not surprisingly, history, particularly colonial history, is the largest single category of presentations at BASAS, 30%. At approximately 20%, history presentations are equally split between the colonial and pre-colonial periods at Wisconsin. EASAS, which eschews pre-colonial topics, is 8% colonial.

Religious Studies. Religious studies comprise 10% of all presentations, hitting a high of 15% at SASA. Fourteen percent of scholars based in the US did religious studies presentation while 7% of West European and only 3% of UK based researchers did so (see Table 9). However, nearly all of these deal with Hinduism and a few with Islam. Buddhism, Jainism, Sikhism, and Christianity and tribal religions were all ignored. This is a very significant oversight.

Cultural Studies. It seems that Americans are the only ones to care about South Asian culture, defined as art, music, ethnomusicology, dance, cinema and literature. Only 17% of all papers dealt with cultural issues; 82% of them were delivered by scholars based in the United States.

Conclusions

A review of hard conference data rather than professional judgment calls leads to both expected and sometimes new perspectives on the state of South Asian studies.

Gaps in Interaction: There is a lot less interaction and networking among scholars than is often assumed. Scholars on each side of the Atlantic tend to stay on their side of the pond. Additional interaction and networking would undoubtedly increase the quantity and quality of research taking place on both sides of the ocean.

Gaps in Resources: There is a significant need for more resources to be directed to economic and political studies. This will be difficult because both fields are currently in the grip of an intellectual fashion which disparages area studies as a path to tenure for younger scholars. This is especially noticeable at Wisconsin, a preferred venue for post-graduate students to explore the academic life. There are almost no economists present and very few political scientists. Yet everyone agrees that India is a rapidly emerging political, military and economic powerhouse.

Gaps in Traction: Religious studies, while popular in the US, have very little traction in Europe. On both sides of the Atlantic, however, religious studies mean Hinduism and sometimes Islam. Other faiths go unrecognized except, possibly, in the context of religious studies conferences. However, a general cultural understanding of South Asia can only be enriched by an increased understanding of the area's religions.

Gaps in Interest: Europeans generally demonstrate a lack of interest in cultural matters, notably the performing and graphic arts. Americans appear to be quite keen on these topics.

Gaps in Commitment: Expatriates are increasingly coming to dominate the field although it is not clear how long this will continue given India's burgeoning economic growth and the current drive to expand Indian higher education. A new college or university is being created every day in India with the expectation that this will continue for the next several years. It is likely to trigger a massive reverse brain-drain comparable to the one currently besetting California's Silicon Valley. While good for India, it inevitably will work to hobble our understanding of the region unless Western universities make a serious, good faith effort to reach out and create exchange relations with their South Asian counterparts. Such cooperation is already widespread and growing rapidly.

Notes

1. Columbia, Cornell - Syracuse Consortium, the Research Triangle Consortium (Duke, North Carolina, North Carolina State), UC-Berkeley, Chicago, Michigan, Texas-Austin, Washington-Seattle, Wisconsin-Madison, Pennsylvania.

2. Elder, Joseph W., Edward C. Dimmock, Jr., Ainslie T. Embree, eds. *India's Worlds and U.S. Scholars, 1947-1997*. New Delhi: Manohar Publishers & Distributors, 1998.

3. *India Review* 5.1 (January, 2006).

4. While well beyond the scope of this essay, to a very real extent this represents a victory for the views of Thomas Kuhn over those of Karl Popper. See, for example, Steve Fuller. *Kuhn vs. Popper: The Struggle for the Soul of Science*. New York: Columbia UP, 2004.

5. Ayres, Alyssa. "India Studies in the United States." *India Review* 5.1 (January, 2006): 21.

6. Adams, John. "Economics, Economists, and the Indian Economy." *India Review* 5.1 (January, 2006): 53-54.

7. The EASAS conference data listed institutional affiliation separately from author and title. A great many presenters were not cross-listed between the two documents. This accounts for the very large number of unknowns in the EASAS dataset.

Dr. William Vanderbok is a retired political scientist, University of California, Los Angeles. As president of the South Asian Studies Association, he represented SASA at the Open Pages conference.

SASA Books is a project of the South Asian Studies Association, a recognized 501(c)3 non-profit, public benefit corporation of scholars and others interested in South Asia.

Using a *pro bono* model, SASA Books is dedicated to publishing high-quality scholarly materials using a rigorous double-blind vetting process.

Both the SASA and SASA Books websites are located at www.sasaonline.org.

www.ingramcontent.com/pod-product-compliance
Lightning Source LLC
Chambersburg PA
CBHW060655100426
42734CB00047B/1827
* 9 7 8 0 9 8 3 4 4 7 2 8 3 *